ACA'S BEGINNER'S GUIDE TO

FLY CASTING

ACA'S BEGINNER'S GUIDE TO

FLY CASTING

FEATURING THE TWELVE CASTS YOU NEED TO KNOW

JOHN L. FIELD

Skyhorse Publishing

Skyhorse Publishing books may be purchased in bulk at special discounts for sales promotion, corporate gifts, fund-raising, or educational purposes. Special editions can also be created to specifications. For details, contact the Special Sales Department, Skyhorse Publishing, 307 West 36th Street, 11th Floor, New York, NY 10018 or info@skyhorsepublishing.com.

Skyhorse® and Skyhorse Publishing® are registered trademarks of Skyhorse Publishing, Inc.®, a Delaware corporation.

Visit our website at www.skyhorsepublishing.com.

10 9 8 7 6 5 4 3 2 1

Library of Congress Cataloging-in-Publication Data is available on file.

Cover design by Tom Lau
Cover photo credit: John L. Field

ISBN: 978-1-5107-2303-0
Ebook ISBN: 978-1-5107-2304-7

Printed in China

To Chris Korich and Steve Rajeff

CONTENTS

Foreword by Steve Rajeff   ix
Preface   xi
Introduction   xiii

Chapter 1   Getting Started   1
     Parts of a Fly-Rod Outfit   5
     Parts of the Reel   6
     Fly Line Manufacture and Design   7
     Leaders   9
     Line Connections   10
     Your First Outfit   12
     Assembling and Disassembling a Fly-Fishing Outfit   14
     Instruction and DIY   17

Chapter 2   A Good Foundation   21
     Stance   22
     The Casting Stroke   22
     Grip   23
     Rod Plane   24
     Rod Stop   24
     Rod Arc and the Loop   24
     False Casts   25
     180-Degree Principle   25
     Trajectory   26
     Timing and Tempo   27
     Going through the Motions   28
     Line Control   29

Chapter 3   Cast Basics   31
     Roll Cast   31
     Pick-Up and Lay-Down   34
     False Cast   35
     Lengthening and Shortening Line (without Hauling)   35
     Hauling Line: Single and Double   36
     Double-Haul False Cast Drill   38
     Shooting Line with Hauls   38
     Wind Casts   39
     Kids   42

Chapter 4	Accuracy	47
	Change-of-Direction Cast	51
Chapter 5	Distance Casting	53
	Wind and Trajectory	53
	Distance Stroke	55
	Release and Shooting Line	59
	Maximum Double-Haul	59
	Using the Body	59
	Shooting Heads	61
	Distance Training	62
Chapter 6	Fishing Casts	65
	Depth and Speed Control in Moving Water	67
	The Saltwater Quick Cast	70
	Equipment Maintenance	72
Chapter 7	Troubleshooting	75
	Poor Timing	76
	Wide Loop Fault	76
	Tailing Loop Fault	78
	Rod Plane (Tracking) Faults	79
	Hauling Faults and Cures	81
	Insufficient Distance	82
Chapter 8	ACA Clubs and Events	83
	ACA-Recognized Fly Events	85
	Fly Accuracy Events	85
	Fly Distance Events	89
	Special Events	90
	Joining and Getting in Touch with the ACA	96
Chapter 9	Exercises for Distance Casting	99
	Glossary	101
	Acknowledgments	103
	Index	105

FOREWORD

The sensation of a solid crack of the bat on a hardball, a perfect smack into a golf ball, a dart toss into the bullseye, the swish through the net from the free throw line, or the release of a perfect fly casting loop are examples of fantastic feelings of things well done. Done right, these activities feel easy, look effortless, and are truly joyful. Learning the basics to form well shaped loops and the casts, needed for success in flyfishing, can be accomplished within weeks, feels easy in months, but may take a lifetime to master. In *The ACA's Beginner's Guide to Fly Casting*, John Field expertly lays out steps to learn and progress through the various casts and techniques needed in fishing, as well as an introduction into tournament casting. Following these steps will greatly accelerate the learning curve to better fly casting and attaining that fun feeling. Tournament casting for me was something that, starting at age ten, required focus on getting a dry fly to land in a small target. My coach said if you can hit the targets, it will make it easier to present a fly more accurately when fishing, and you will catch more fish. More than fifty years later, I can wholeheartedly confirm it is true: A high degree of accuracy casting skill will help catch more fish. Also, in forms of fishing where long casts play an important role, learning techniques for competition distance events translates into greater catches. A great thing about fly casting and fishing, is that it can be learned at any age, and will present challenges and chances to improve all along the journey.

In writing this book, John draws from a lifetime of angling and more than fifteen years supporting tournament casting in the United States. He served as American Casting Association President and was my line tender (ghillie) in Fly Distance events for several Nationals. He was my ghillie when I broke the ACA Single Hand Distance record of 243 feet in 2009 in Mississauga, Ontario. I could hardly walk due to a knee injury, but the adrenaline kicked in and I had the strength to make the perfect distance cast. During a casting tournament co-sponsored by IGFA/ACA in 2008 in Florida, which John coordinated, an amusing incident occurred. We had rented a large grass field from a county parks and recreation department to conduct a distance competition, but when we showed up at 7:30 a.m., the field was covered with five thousand cars—overflow from a bigger than expected charity 5K running event! When we calmed down, we joked that at least we had a good spectator turnout. A field nearby, where radio-controlled airplanes were buzzing and jetting around noisily, sufficed and we still conducted the distance events.

Having been in casting competitions and on several fishing trips with John, he has a highly-tuned sense of mechanics and has artfully applied them to the easy-to-follow descriptions and step-by-step instructions within these pages. Read, practice, and have fun!

—Steve Rajeff

PREFACE

This is the small book that legendary angling author, editor, and publisher Nick Lyons initially asked me to write for his son Tony Lyon's then-fledgling publishing company almost ten years ago. Hoping to maximize the public relations potential for the American Casting Association, I went a little overboard and presented an outline for a book that threw a much wider net. The book was put on hold for a few years but then Nick asked me to proceed and the result was a bigger, advanced casting book titled *Fly-Casting Finesse*. After finishing that project, I revisited the original concept and wrote *ACA's Beginner's Guide to Fly Casting*, as the prequel to the first book.

INTRODUCTION

This book intends to teach the American Casting Association's method of learning how to cast efficiently, so you can be effective and enjoy your fishing or tournament casting. The book starts with advice on selecting your first fly rod and how to set it up and care for it. Next, this book explains the ACA method using a unified method of casting developed in tournament casting and fishing. Chris Korich has been immensely helpful by recently distilling these methods for me to share in this book. I will give advice on how to learn on your own, at clubs, or with mentors and professional instructors.

You will learn a good foundation for making the fundamental casts, then focus on having the control to cast accurately and cast to your maximum distance. Since the fundamentals of ACA's methods aim at tournament casting, I will show you how to use these casts in fishing situations in fresh and saltwater with specific types of presentation in mind, and give advice on how to cope with the challenges of windy conditions.

Since no one is perfect, I included a chapter on troubleshooting the cast which explains what to look for and how to make corrections. At the end of the book, there is also a casting glossary of the some common terms for your reference. If you are in good health and really want to unlock your distance casting potential, read the exercises for distance. Please consult your physician or trainer before performing them.

In Chapter 8, ACA Clubs and Events (page 83), there is a description of the fly events and a club directory. You will find here the rules for the popular 5wt event, which is a good starter event for any local fishing club or fishing-related organization or promotion. Most of us like to catch fish, but others enjoy casting better. It's totally up to you.

CHAPTER 1

GETTING STARTED

A fly is a hand-crafted representation of a food or threat that fish consume or attack. Some fish are carnivorous and others are vegetarians. When fish strike something, it is usually motivated by hunger, but often it's just instinctive or learned behavior. When fish spawn they are often territorial and attack parasitic or predatory intruders. With salmon and trout, spawning suppresses appetite, so striking at flies is mainly a reflexive feeding behavior. The stomachs of spawning salmon are usually empty, yet anglers catch them on flies.

The size of the creatures that a fish will bite—and that we can imitate with flies—ranges from almost microscopic to about sixteen inches in length. The maximum size of a fly an angler might use is limited by his or her ability to cast it. Someone who designs their own flies has the choice of creating a realistic, an artistic, or an impressionistic imitation of what the fly tier thinks the prey might be. You tie a fly by attaching man-made or natural materials to a hook shank, tube, or line with thread and/or adhesives. Depending on the tier's objective, hook weight, materials, and quantities, flies can be made to sit on top of the water, just below, or sink at varying rates.

Fly fishing is generally harder to learn and perform than conventional fishing with bait or lures. It is considered by most anglers to be more challenging, and to have fewer impacts on a fishery. Many fly anglers voluntarily use barbless hooks to minimize damage to fish. With large flies imitating finned prey, tiers seldom use more than one hook. That is much less damaging than the three-treble hooks on many crankbaits used with spin or conventional tackle. Flies are also usually safer to fish because they lodge in the fish's mouth, whereas fish tend to swallow live and artificial baits deeper, where the hooks can cause more damage.

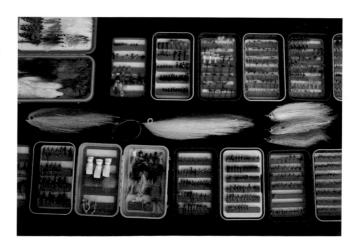

This is an assortment of weighted flies, floating flies, and poppers to catch a variety of freshwater and saltwater fish on or below the surface.

In conventional fishing, baits or lures vary in weight from around 1/8 ounce, up to several pounds in the case of live saltwater bait. Flies tend to be lighter to facilitate easier casting. In either case, the translucent monofilament line is usually undetectable by the fish. In terms of simple machine mechanics, all fishing rods are a combination of lever and spring, but you cast them differently.

When an angler casts a bait or lure with a spinning or bait-casting outfit, she leaves the bait or lure hanging by the line a few inches or feet below the rod tip and pins the line to the grip or holds it with a button. Then she makes a cast with the rod which bends the rod and throws the projectile when she releases the line or button. The momentum of the bait or lure pulls the line off the spool of the reel until it lands. When you catch a fish, or wish to bring in a bait or lure, you crank the line back on the reel with the handle. It is to be taken for granted these reels will have various drag systems to allow a big fish to pull line off the spool without breaking the main fishing line. With spinning and bait-casting reels, the handle does not spin backward when the line goes out. It remains stationary.

In fly fishing, the fly is relatively light and the relatively heavy line provides the weight needed to deliver the fly to its target. To prevent the fish from associating the heavy line with the fly, we use a leader or tippet made out of a translucent monofilament. When you fish for species with certain kinds of teeth, you would use other materials such as steel to prevent the fish from biting through the leader.

To make a cast with a fly rod, you need some line extended beyond the rod tip in a manner that provides resistance (I'll teach this shortly) and then you must accelerate the rod with a stroke to get the line moving towards where you want it to go, then stop the rod to control the formation of an unrolling loop which will move toward its aimed direction. The bend in the rod is an indication of the result of your stroke against the line's resistance in relation to the flexibility of the rod.

The American Fishing Tackle Trade Association publishes a line-weight chart showing the standard for lines from a 1-weight to a 15-weight. Weight is abbreviated as wt., or indicated with the # symbol. The measurement, typically in grain weight (or 1/7000ths of a pound), is made for the first thirty feet of the line, starting at the tip where the leader would connect. Line manufacturers also measure and offer lines with just the grain weight of the first thirty feet. The fly-rod industry tries to design and label rods to correspond to these line weights. Most manufacturers are now laser marking the line information on the line coating of beginning of the fly line.

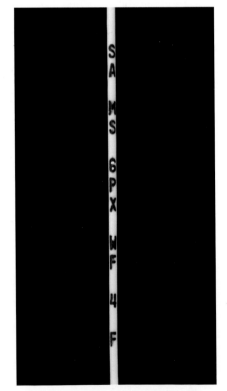

These marks indicate that this is a Scientific Anglers Mastery Series GPX model weight-forward 4-weight floating fly line.

The rod acts as part lever and part spring. The action of a fly rod is how much the rod will bend and where it will bend against a downward pull, or resistance, on its tip. Rod designers and builders have testing equipment for this and measure and record rod actions. Rod manufacturers usually design a rod with an intended purpose and an action to achieve it. The action of a rod is designed to assist in casting well at distances, presentation, and in also protecting the tippet—the thin, translucent, and weakest part of the line attached to the fly.

The descriptors currently used in marketing rods to describe rod actions are slow, medium, and fast. A slow action bends from the tip all the way into the grip, a medium action from about half way down to the tip, and a fast action rod bends mainly from the tip to about a third of the way down.

Although it isn't the best choice for all-round accuracy and distance, a slow-action rod is easier to cast for beginners, and it can help maintain tension, so the hook can be set and you can detect soft bites. A medium-action rod is a good compromise for accuracy, presentation, and distance. A fast-action rod is intended for heavy flies and casting distance, but not intended for light tippets. The action of a rod also has an influence on how you cast them, but I'll get more into that later.

When you cast a fly toward the fish, or where you suspect a fish to be, there are two ways to make the cast reach. Either you pull line off the reel as you add more and more length in the air while you casting back and forth until it is the right length and make your delivery, or you have line ready and release it into a cast so its weight pulls line through the rod guides. The latter is like throwing an apple off a stick. These steps have specific names and techniques which I'll describe in detail in this book.

Instead of retrieving a fly every cast by cranking the reel handle, as you would on a spinning or bait-casting reel, you use your line hand (the one you don't cast with) and pull line back in through the guides. This action is called stripping line in. You can also strip line out, by pulling it off the reel.

When you catch a small fish, you can strip the line to bring the fish in and even let the fish pull line back through your fingers if necessary. If you catch a bigger fish that could break the line against resistance, it's usually safer to reel-in the slack and fight the fish "on the reel" to prevent a break off from tangles. In some instances you must make sure a furiously-spinning handle doesn't hit you in the knuckles, and there are few fly reels made with special anti-reverse mechanisms to prevent this. Most reels today have an adjustable mechanical drag to control for this purpose and I'll describe it more later on in the book.

There are different reasons why people fish. It can provide a challenge, immersion in nature, friendly competition between anglers, or a means of providing food. Some anglers want to catch the most fish in the least amount of time, others want to catch the biggest fish they can. Anglers can select the type of tackle they use based on the degree of challenge or to minimize the impact on the environment. Tackle can even impact the likelihood a fish will survive being caught and released. Worms catch trout readily but cause them to swallow the hook and die. Some anglers harvest all the fish they catch when permitted and others catch and release most or all they catch. In some places where harvesting isn't permitting you must release every caught fish with the least injury and stress.

Fly casting and fly fishing have their unique rewards. You can catch most fish with bait and lures on bait or spin tackle more easily, but when you catch them on a fly rod, the degree of difficulty is higher. Most fly anglers say it is more fun to play fish on a fly rod because having the handle near the end is a disadvantage; it's more challenging. A fly rod gives good feedback through the grip when we cast well. If you golf or play tennis, you might have had a similar experience with a club or racquet. The best fly fishing is experienced pursuing wild fish in beautiful places. A nicely-cast loop is beautiful to see sailing through the air anywhere. Do it in the wild and it's even more special.

As the name of this book states, it's intended for people who are just beginning to cast a fly rod. You may never have fished before with any type of tackle, or you may have used other tackle and want to add fly fishing to widen your repertoire or increase your fishing skills. There are several key things you need to know to become a successful fly fisher: What equipment and flies to use, how to cast and present a fly, and where and when to fish. This small book offers the very basics of how to cast and a primer on presentation. If you want to read about advanced fly casting and presentation, get a hardcover or digital copy of my book *Fly-Casting Finesse: A Complete Guide to Improving All Aspects of Your Casting* (Skyhorse Publishing, 2015).

Sight fishing is when you can see one or more fish, or the effect of their movement in the wild, and present your fly to them in an enticing manner. The most challenging is fishing for one individual fish, instead of casting into or in front of a group or school. Casting accuracy is important because if the fish you want does not see the fly, it won't take it, but if you hit the fish on the head it will usually spook. Timing is also critical. If the fish is cycling around a pool or structure, or establishes a feeding rhythm, putting the fly down when it isn't ready will result in failure.

If the water is clear, you can usually see the fish's reaction to your fly, or if it's muddy, you might see signs of a quick exit. It will either spook, strike, follow and strike, follow and refuse, or ignore your offering completely. It's exciting to see an immediate take, but it is very helpful to see other reactions so you can change what you're doing to increase your success! If you like to sight fish, fly fishing is ideal.

The other types of fly fishing where distance casting is very important are structure fishing, fan casting, chumming, and teasing. Structure fishing is when you cast close to a shoreline, island, or over submerged structure. It can also be casting to places in moving water where an unseen fish might be located. Fan casting is when you make long casts at regular intervals in a semi-circle resembling a Chinese fan. Chumming is when you throw food in the water and cast to the fish that come to feed. Teasing and "bait and switch," is when another person casts or trolls a hook-less bait or lure until fish show up. Then the person doing the teasing withdraws the teaser and the angler casts a fly to the fish. All of these require accurate casts, except fan casting.

PARTS OF A FLY-ROD OUTFIT

Lightweight fly rods for freshwater fish feature an end cap at the butt end made of aluminum, plastic, or rubber to protect the end of the rod if it contacts ground or pavement. On saltwater rods meant for large fish, there is usually a fighting butt below the reel to place in contact with your stomach or thigh as a pivot while fighting large fish. This fighting butt is an extension of about three inches with cork or soft rubber.

The next part is called the reel seat and holds the reel onto the rod aligned with the guides. There are two systems of locking real seats. The first is the up-locking seat and the second is the down-locking seat. The up-locking seat is the most common. There is one advantage to a down-locking seat for freshwater use or tournament casting—there are fewer items below the reel for line to catch on, but there is no fighting butt.

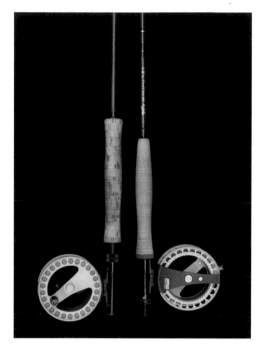

Here are down-locking (left) and up-locking (right) reel seats showing where your hand grips the handle in relation to the end of the rods.

Rod manufacturers use three main handle shapes, full-wells, reverse half-wells (often called Western), and cigar. The idea is, the larger the line weight and the more effort needed for casting or fighting fish, the more thumb support is needed. Therefore, most manufacturers install full-wells handles for rods over 7 weight and half-wells or cigar handles for lower line weights. They are even making some of these handle shapes in a range of sizes to fit all needs.

The blank of a rod is the flexible conical-shaped tube on which a fly rod

CIGAR

HALF-WELLS

FULL-WELLS

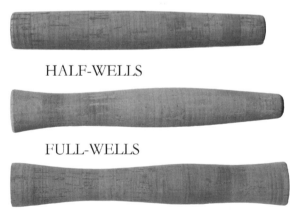

Various cork handle shapes. Due to the increasing scarcity of cork, more handles are being molded of foam materials.

is finished by attaching the other components. Manufacturers make them out of tapered man-made composites like graphite or of cultivated split-bamboo cane and glue. Rodmakers roll the blank material for modern graphite fly rods on a steel mandrel of the same length as the rod.

For ease of shipping to the dealers and transport by the consumer, rodmakers cut the rods into shorter lengths and fit them with mating ferrules for disassembly and reassembly. Some manufacturers offer one-piece rods for economy and decreased maintenance. With few exceptions, rods are available in two-piece through four-piece. Today, four-piece rods are the most commonly available.

Rods usually have a label on the rod blank. It usually states the make and model, as well as line weight and length. Older rods were even marked with their physical weight. Most composite rod makers today coat the blank in pigmented epoxy. All windings on rods for decoration or attachment and labels are covered in a protective clear epoxy or varnish. A hook-keeper, essentially a loop of formed stainless wire, is normally attached above the handle for hanging your fly when you're not using it.

To control the fly-line with the rod and minimize friction, the line must be threaded and travel through rod guides which are attached to the rod at calculated intervals. The guides attach at one or two points and have either an integral ring surface in the case of wire guides, or a ring insert made of hard smooth metal ceramic alloys. The guides on earlier rods featured polished agate stone.

The first guides the line passes through are the largest in diameter and help straighten the line. The first guide is called the stripper guide. Next there are usually a few ring or circular guides, then snake guides, and the tip guide at the end of the rod. Snakes are coiled wire forming a loop with flattened attachment feet. The diameter of the guides is progressively smaller toward the tip. The tip guide is a ring attached at about a 30-degree angle to a tapered tube. This guide fits over the tip end of the blank and attached by hot glue.

PARTS OF THE REEL

The main parts of a fly reel are the frame, spool, foot, handle, drag, and clicker. The clicker makes a *clicking* or *zipping* sound and adds friction to the spool to prevent overruns when there is no other drag mechanism. Some clickers are adjustable and some are not. In the case of those that are not adjustable, the resistance is usually below the breaking strength of most tippets. The sound of a clicker helps an angler and a guide hear whether line is going out or not.

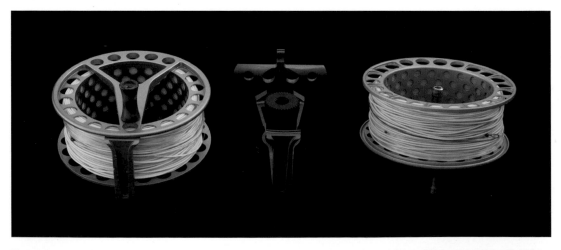

The reel and quick interchange spools shown here are very convenient so you can have different weights, densities, lengths, and designs of fly lines at a moment's notice when your needs change.

The clicker sounds when an angler strips line off the spool, when a fish runs, or when a fly is snagged and the angler is moving away in another direction.

There are also more positive mechanisms and techniques to deter a willful fish from taking your line or reaching entanglements. On some reels there is a palming rim on the edge of the spool for your reel hand to add friction. The most effective mechanism, however, is an adjustable internal drag system incorporating friction washers or metallic cone designs. These can also be used in conjunction with stripping-in and palming. In big-game fly reels, the clicker serves more as a signal to the angler, guide, or crew about the actions of a running fish. The maximum size fish taken on specialized fly tackle today is about five hundred pounds!

Most of today's reels have one-piece frames and removable spools of either molded graphite composite or machined aluminum. The removable spool gives you the option of getting extras for additional lines. Anglers often have at least a sinking line and a floating line, for example. In a well-designed reel, the spool can be changed in seconds.

FLY LINE MANUFACTURE AND DESIGN

To provide strength, manufacturers build fly lines on a core of single- or multifilament fiber. The core then usually has a smooth plastic-like coating, so a finished line can slip through the guides and your fingers with little friction. The designers choose the density of the coating and additives to make a line either floating or sinking, and in the case of sinking lines, they specify variations for line density and sink rates.

To increase the weight of the line built on the light core and to control stiffness, manufacturers regulate the thicknesses of coating along the length of the line. Changes in line diameter are called taper. The total weight is engineered for different rod weights. The taper changes the

FLY LINE TAPERS

Level Taper- L

Double Taper- DT

Weight Forward Taper with integrated running line- WF

Weight Forward Compound Taper with integrated running line- WF

Shooting head (tapered) and Shooting line- SH

Triangle Taper with integrated running line

These line tapers are designed for various purposes having to do with how well they cast at different distances, how well they roll cast and how well they will present a fly.

weight distribution and the way the line transfers energy down the line and leader during a cast. Thin line lands softly but doesn't have as much mass as a thicker section. In addition to tapered fly lines, level fly lines—with a single line width the entire length of the fly line—are also available.

There are four basic taper designs that vary in diameter over their length. The first taper is called the double taper. The front half and back halves of the lines are mirror images of each other and can be reversed to extend the life of the line. The double taper starts with a thin level tip section about six inches. Next is a taper of constant angle, like a cone, which starts at the back end of the tip and increases in diameter, typically for about six feet in length. This blends into a section of level line called the belly. The belly contains most of the line weight we cast with. In the case of the double taper, the belly is double length and ends at the rear taper which starts with the same diameter as that of the belly and decreases in diameter until another tip section. The tapers provide a smooth transition and more, which we'll cover later. If we attached the leader directly to the line's thick belly, it would hit the water harder than we'd usually prefer.

Weight-forward lines have a tip, a front taper, a belly and a rear taper. The rear taper which is usually about the same angle and length as the front taper, ends at a level running line which comprises the remainder of the line. The running line is about half the diameter of the belly, for several reasons. This thinnest line takes up less room on the reel spool and reduces friction through the guides and resistance in the air. The running line also acts like the tail on a kite when long casts are made. Since the head is over forty feet, you may wonder when and how does the running line come out? This will be covered in shooting and other techniques. The rear taper is a smooth transition in diameter between the belly and the running line. It helps smooth out certain types of casts which you will later learn.

A compound taper is a weight-forward line whose tapers or belly don't have constant angles. These are designed with more weight concentrated where the designer wants it. Usually a compound taper has more weight in the front of the belly or front taper, so it will theoretically cast better at short distances, without affecting long-distance casts. A short head is better to turn over heavy or wind-resistant flies and a long head delays turnover and is better for long casts with flies of most sizes.

The Triangle taper has a tip and combines a gradual front taper and belly up to a normal back taper. The heads are available in varying lengths. This design has most of the weight rearward and closer to the rod tip which is slightly better for roll casts than overhead casts.

The line from the front tip to the end of the running line is called the head. Even if the line differs in diameter along its length, if it has a continuous core with a running line, it is referred to as an integrated line. Another type of weight-forward line is a shooting line. Shooting lines consist of a head connected or knotted to a shooting line of much smaller diameter. The shooting line serves the same purpose as a running line but there are more choices in diameter, strength, and material and they are replaceable.

Backing is a thinner and lighter line connected or knotted to the back end of a fly line that can serve two purposes. First, it can be used to fill the spool to provide the largest possible spool arbor diameter, which maximizes the length of line retrieved with each turn of the reel handle. Secondly, it increases the length of the line in the event a large fish makes a run longer than your line. This prevents a sudden break-off when the line comes tight. The most common material for backing is braided Dacron because it is the least likely to cause a line burn to your fingers if you try to apply finger pressure to the line. Ideally, the breaking strength of the backing should be equal to, or greater than that of the fly line core.

LEADERS

The object of a leader is to reduce the visibility of the fly line near the fly, so that fish are not scared away. The other equally-important purpose of the leader is to reduce the energy of the line so it lands more softly than the bare fly line would. Fish like trout do not feed when they see or feel unnatural objects fall hard from the sky or go swimming by!

Making a leader less visible than the fly line is also accomplished by using clear or tinted monofilament nylon or fluorocarbon line. You match the tint to the water color. There are green, coffee and clear tippet material. The diameter of leader material for freshwater is usually measured in the X system. This system refers to diameter, but breaking strength varies by many factors. For example, 5X leader tippet is supposed to be .006 inches diameter and 4 pound test, but nominally might measure .0055 inches and test 4.5 pounds. Here are the line diameter and lb. test formulas for the X system:

$$11\text{-diameter in thousandths of an inch} = X \text{ rating}$$
$$11\text{-X rating} = \text{diameter in thousandths of an inch}$$
$$9\text{-X rating} = \text{test weight in pounds}$$

For example, 11 − .006 inches = 5X rating; 11 − 5X = .006 inches diameter, and 9 − 5X = 4 pound. test. Most saltwater fishermen, on the other hand, prefer to use break strength instead when constructing leaders. For example, you might use a 20-pound test tippet average for striped bass and twelve for bonefish.

There are generally three sections of a leader. The part of the leader you attach to a fly line is called the butt section. It is nearly as thick as the tip of the fly line and should be about as flexible. The next section is the midsection which should be thinner and of less strength and the last is the tippet. The tippet is usually the thinnest, weakest section and can be lengthened to around three feet to make the midsection less visible. When designing a leader for fish with close-mesh teeth like bluefish or pike, a bite-tippet of heavy mono or wire attached to the fly might be necessary, and for these species, stealth is usually not compromised because they generally aren't "line shy."

A leader can be hand-tied lengths of different diameter material, or machine-made down to a level tippet or bite-tippet connection, of knotless tapered-leader material.

The way to make a smooth transition from the thick fly line to the end of the leader is to taper the diameter of the material down toward the fly. A short leader turns over hard and a longer one turns over more slowly. When you first learn to cast, the object is to have the leader land fully extended after the cast. So, abruptness of taper, final diameter, and length are the basic design considerations. One more factor, not as obvious, is the stiffness of the material selected. This will influence how well the leader will unroll when you cast.

When you are just learning or practicing, use a tippet heavy enough so you won't be breaking off too often. For practice a 10- to 15-pound test tippet is fine but when trout fishing, you might be using four pounds on average. The characteristics of a fishing leader should depend on the species you're pursuing and the conditions you're fishing in. The leader might need to be undetectable, designed to turn over easily, provide slack, or require protection from bite-offs. You can buy ready-made leaders or tie your own. You can select the dimensions, taper, and materials in your leader.

Nylon and fluorocarbon are today's two leader material choices. I opt for nylon for fresh water floating presentations, but will use a fluorocarbon tippet or replace the tippets of worn knotless nylon leaders with fluorocarbon, without worries of losing the floating properties of the fly. Nylons from different brands and selections can vary greatly in stiffness and you should use this to your advantage when designing a leader.

You can buy ready-made saltwater leaders or tie your own (or better yet, use your guide's leaders if you are fishing with one). For saltwater fish, I almost always use fluorocarbon rather than nylon. Fluorocarbon is stellar because it has much higher abrasion resistance than nylon with a greater strength-to-diameter ratio. Therefore, an angler can use thinner tipper diameters when stealth counts. When fluorocarbon first came out, I tried to cut a tag end with my teeth like I used to with nylon. It was so hard it hurt!

In fly fishing, choosing, testing, combining, and tuning the right components can create well-matched equipment and prepare you for the field. This will help you be more efficient in performing casts and fishing more intuitively. The ultimate goal in fly-casting is to learn the feel of all types of fly rods and line combinations and if presented with an unfamiliar outfit, adapt your stroke to make good casts.

LINE CONNECTIONS

If your reel did not come with backing and line attached and loaded on the spool, you, another person, or your local fly shop must do it before you can start. It's always hard to estimate how much backing to use but there is a trick to getting it right. Tape the end of the fly line to the spool and wind it on. Next, do the same with the start of the backing and evenly wind it on until it is about 3/8-inch from the top of the spool. Take the backing off in an open field or put in on a temporary spool and do the same thing with the fly line.

Then attach and wind the backing first onto the fly reel spool using the following instructions. The backing comes in bulk spools and must be attached to the arbor of the reel spool so you can wind it onto the spool without slipping and with the correct tension so it won't dig into itself under strain. If a fish takes all your line, connecting the end to the spool may or may not save it and the fish. However, a favorable and lucky outcome has occurred this way on many occasions.

You can either hold the loose reel while loading it, or attach it to the lower rod section. If you do, it may be easier if you thread the backing through the stripper guide. One easy way to tie the end of the backing to the reel spool is with a knot called the Arbor Knot. Pass the end of the backing twice around the arbor and tie an Overhand knot around the standing line. Next tighten the standing line until the knot is near the arbor and pull the tag end until it's snug. Continue pulling the standing line until the

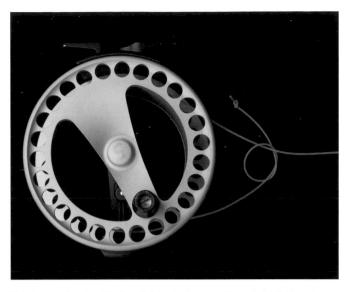

This is an arbor knot before tightening on a reel set for right-hand wind. If your reel is set up for left hand wind, insert the line through the other side.

knot jams against the arbor. Trim, leaving 3/16 inch and wind on your backing.

Stores with a line machine can quickly load your reel with backing and line or you must load it yourself. You can mount the reel on the reel seat and hold onto the lower rod half while you wind or just hold onto the reel foot and frame. While reeling, use your finger tips and guide the line back and forth to keep it level like the level-wind in a conventional reel.

The fly line must next be connected to the backing. Most modern fly-lines come with a rear welded loop for this purpose. This loop can also be used to attach shooting lines which I'll cover later. To attach it and leave the flexibility of detaching your line without cutting anything, you can use a connection called the Handshake Loop. First tie a Double Surgeon's Loop in the backing large enough to easily pass the reel or fly line spool through.

The way to tie it is to double the backing, making a loop about 14 inches long, and tie an Overhand Knot just about the point where the line is double but pass the end with the loop through the Overhand Knot twice and tighten; leaving the Surgeon's Loop. To connect this to

the fly-line, insert the end of the Surgeon's Loop into the welded fly line loop and put the line on the spool or the reel through this loop. Then tighten the connection until the loops tighten in the manner in the photo.

Now you're ready to attach the leader to the fly line. Most lines today come with a welded front loop for this purpose. If you

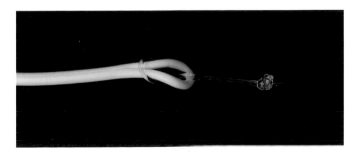

This is the fly line and leader connected with a hand-shake, or loop-to-loop connection. It is also used to join tippets to the leader. This system enables you to change leaders or tippets in a hurry for whatever reason.

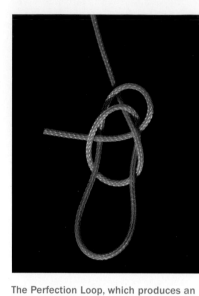

The Perfection Loop, which produces an elegant single-strand loop usually used in loop-to-loop connections.

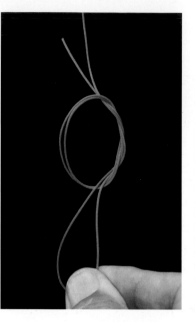

This is the Surgeon's Loop. The standard knot produces a single-strand loop, but if you make the loop long enough, you can tie another Surgeon's Loop with it and create a four-strand loop. All you have to do to tie it is make a loop about a foot long and use it to make a double overhand knot and tighten, trim the tag. The standard knot passes through twice, but if you pass through three times, it's a triple Surgeon's Loop for added strength.

tie a loop in the butt of your leader you can connect or disconnect them in seconds. The Perfection Loop is my preferred knot for this. The second would be the double Surgeon's Loop which is slightly bulkier and often not as straight. The object is to tie a loop about ¾ inch in length so you can connect the leader and line with a Handshake Loop, as I described for the backing to line connection.

If your fly line lacks a loop or it gets damaged, replace it with a Nail Knot. You can attach your leader directly to the fly line, or you

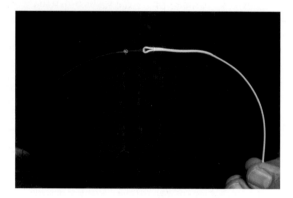

The butt end of this leader and the tip of the fly line have similar flexibility so the line will be able to properly turn over the leader. Photo: Edina Field.

can use the Nail Knot and attach a six- to twelve-inch piece of mono about the thickness of the leader butt. Tie a loop on the other end of it to connect to the leader loop. I cut off factory loops and do this anyway because I think it helps the cast a little.

The line-to-leader connections, as well as leader-to-butt selection, should not cause hinging, or excessive stiffness. Poor leader connections can interrupt the energy transfer from the line to the leader.

YOUR FIRST OUTFIT

Everyone can learn to cast a fly rod. It's easier to start with a rod measuring seven-feet, six inches, to eight feet, six inches in length than with a standard nine-foot rod. For kids, the shorter the better. A rule of thumb is that the rod should be no longer than one and a half times the height of small casters. I recommend that everyone, regardless of strength and size, start with a matched 4- or 5-weight outfit consisting of a floating line, leader, rod, and reel. This size will also be matched to fish most small- to medium-sized freshwater cold and warm water species. Beginners are best off learning to cast and fish with a medium-action rod. Stay away from stiff, fast-action rods made for distance when learning the basics.

Echo fly-rod designer and incredible caster Tim Rajeff suggests that beginners use lines that are designated one or two sizes heavier than the rod designation to make the rod bend more for more feel. He is a big believer in learning by feel, or kinesthetics. When the beginner advances, they can use lighter lines that are more optimal. Many fly shops have bargain bins with inexpensive lines which are good for experimentation.

Since lines are generally less expensive than rods, Tim prefers to "overline" rods when getting started, instead of buying a soft-action rod just to learn on, and then have problems later when fishing in wind or casting longer distances, which are conditions where a stiffer rod is preferable.

Once an angler learns the basics, they can advance to outfits designed for heavier lines if they want to fish for bigger fish and in bigger waters. The most popular length for bigger waters is a 9-inch rod. You can purchase an inexpensive combination outfit for under $200 at the time of this printing. The inexpensive reels you find in a kit will be fine for small freshwater fish, but when you anticipate fish over about five pounds, a better drag system would be helpful or even essential.

Most ready-to-use outfits are set up for left-hand wind but if you select your own components you have a choice. There has always been a debate about which hand to use for reeling. Almost all reels need to be set up by a shop or owner for which direction the drag or clicker will operate. At least one manufacturer builds them permanently in one direction or the other. The debate centers on whether to reel with your dominant or non-dominant hand.

If you can reel line in faster with your dominant hand and you're planning to fight fish that take more than seventy-five yards of line, it might be to your advantage to have reel that retrieves with your dominant hand. If you do, you would have to change hands after hooking a fish, and hold the rod with your non-dominant hand. To begin casting and fishing for smaller fish, I would recommend casting with your dominant hand and a reel set to retrieve with the other.

This is a 6-weight fly-rod outfit including rod, reel, line, and leader for trout and bass. Several makers offer similar entry-level kits in varying sizes. Photo: Edina Field.

These mass-produced rods are usually made with a graphite composite blank, then the components such as the guides, seat, and handle are attached to it. Besides the outfit, there are some tools and accessories you should have on day one.

When practicing casting (which you should never do with a real fly), wear a baseball cap to shield your eyes from sun and sunglasses to protect them injury from the practice fly and knots. I recently was hit in the eye while casting, after I removed my sunglasses when clouds blocked the sun during an accuracy event. It was very painful and could have scratched my eye or worse. I'll bring my yellow sun glasses next time. If you have difficulties focusing on small objects close-up, I recommend glasses with magnification for tying knots or fly tying. I like the functionally of the split magnetic readers with built-in neck loop.

To be able to cut leader material and trim knots, buy a line clipper or carry an extra finger-nail clipper. The stainless-steel line clipper I carry has a retractable bodkin which is like a heavy needle. It's used to remove glue from hook eyes or pick out wind knots from the leader. If you're using a dry fly, buy a bottle of fly floatant to help prevent your fly from sinking. I also recommend using fly ferrule wax or just rubbing some candle wax on the male graphite or fiberglass ferrules on a new rod or after periodically cleaning an older one.

ASSEMBLING AND DISASSEMBLING A FLY-FISHING OUTFIT

You can carry a rod in a tube or rod bag in a car, plane, or backpack and have it ready to fish in minutes. But if these multi-piece rods are not handled properly, breakage or stuck ferrules can result. The main thing is to keep the ferrules out of the dirt.

To assemble a fiberglass or graphite composite rod, take the rod sock, or bag, out of the rod tube and remove the rod sections. Hold the rod sections or place them where they don't get dirty or roll away. Put the bag back in the tube so it doesn't get dirty or wet. If your rod has more than two pieces, continue until you are done, trying not to rest the rod on the ground. A companion could hold it, or rest the butt on a soft spot like grass or the bed of your vehicle.

If you have a four-piece rod, you can assemble the lower sections and upper sections, then join them at the middle ferrule. Start putting it together with the butt section in your non-dominant hand and gently insert the male

This is an angler's-eye view of assembling the ferrules on a composite rod, starting with the rod eyes on the loose rod sections at ninety degree angles apart. Photo: Edina Field.

end into the female ferrule of the next section with your dominant hand, so the guides of the bottom section are facing up and the guides of the next section are at a right angle to the guides of the lower rod section.

Set the assembled lower rod sections down and assemble the other half in the same manner. Next assemble the two halves in the middle by also gently inserting the male end into the female ferrule of the next section so the guides of the bottom section are at a right angle to the next section. Push them together with both hands while twisting them into alignment. To be exact, sight down the guides as if they were gunsights and make any adjustments. In some cases the rod manufacturer will provide alignment marks to facilitate this procedure.

If you have a split-cane bamboo rod, do not insert the ferrules at right angles or twist the rod in any way. This can break the natural fibers. Only push the ferrules of a bamboo rod together aligned or pull the ferrules straight apart.

Next comes the reel. Start attaching the reel by loosening the reel seat locking rings so there is enough room to insert your reel seat. Insert one end into the pocket on the seat that is stationary. If you have an up-locking seat, it will be the top end by the handle. If you have a down-locking seat, it will be the bottom end of the seat. Next, slide the seat hood over the other reel foot and tighten the locking rings until hand tight. If the reel is a little wiggly, you can tap the reel into the stationary pocket with the heel of your hand and retighten.

You may string the rod before or after attaching a leader. To start stringing the rod, thread the end of the leader or line through the opening in the reel frame so the line will have an unobstructed path to the lowest and first guide on the rod called the stripper guide. Next, pull out a length of line from the reel that's a little longer than your rod. Next, double the line about two feet from the end and pinch it between your index and thumb so it forms a tight loop extending about two inches past your finger and thread it through the guides.

When you pull the loop through and one side of the loop is tight to the reel, pull the other one through the tip. Now you can attach a leader or fly, or secure the end or leader so you can move about without tangling or hooking something unintended. If you are attaching a fly, for now it should be a practice fly without a hook. When you take a knotless tapered leader out to uncoil it, there is a simple way to prevent a snarl. Put the fingers of your line hand inside the coil to act as a spool and start unrolling the butt end and use the straightening directions below until the whole leader is ready.

You can string a rod quickly by inserting a loop of line in the guides, instead of sticking the end of the line or leader into the guides like threading a needle. Photo: Edina Field.

Whenever I see coil memory or kinking in a leader, I stretch the sections between my hands by holding it with a loose wrap so my grip doesn't add kinks. I pull almost to the breaking point for each section and then release. Knotless leaders also make straightening easy by pinching the line between thumb and index finger and slowly creating heat with friction by pulling down the leader toward the end. Maintain the stretch for a few

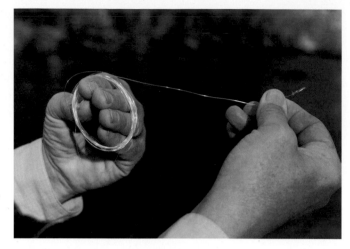

Holding a coiled leader with your finger inside while unrolling it prevents a tangled mess. Photo: Edina Field.

seconds so the leader can cool, then release. A straight leader prevents the fly from springing back and piling.

After stringing the rod, either hold onto the practice fly or secure it. Put the tippet around the reel or put it between the Velcro of the reel bag, otherwise gravity will unthread your rod for you. The same thing happens when you're fishing with flies with hooks. It's best to attach a fly to the hook-keeper or a guide foot after you've strung the rod. Whether you're learning to cast or actually fishing, an Improved Clinch Knot is a very reliable knot. Although you might not be fighting a fish when practicing, you might need a good knot if you need to pull on the line to free it from a snagged weed or branch.

There are two types of practice flies, one made by knotting on a piece of Glo-bug yarn, and a second made by tying on a hook and snipping off the hook at the bend while at the

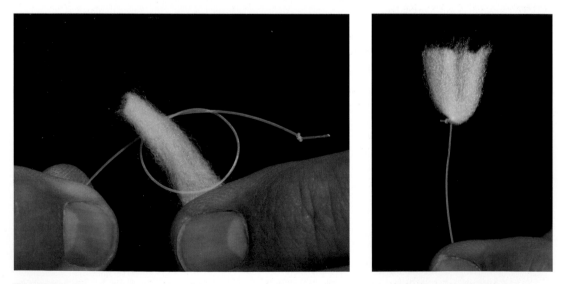

This super-quick yarn knot attaches Glo-bug yarn to your tippet for practice without the danger of a hook. It's actually a mini version of the arbor knot. Photo: Edina Field.

tying bench. A Yarn-fly knot is unsurprisingly good use for yarn flies. The knot starts by tying an overhand knot at the very end of the tippet and tightening it. Next, tie another overhand knot about an inch up but leave it loose and slip the yarn into it with half sticking out either side. Now tighten it in the middle of the yarn until the line slips down and the knot at the end jams against it.

These are the Official Flies of the ACA, clockwise from the upper left corner: Dry Fly Accuracy, Distance, Bass Bug Accuracy, Wet Fly Accuracy, and Trout Fly Accuracy.

For the second type of practice fly, you can use rooster hackle, or Glo-bug yarn tied on a hook shank. I like chartreuse Glo-bug yarn for all-around visibility. I use a dark color on snow or ice. Dress the hook in a tying vise, then cut off the shank at the hook bend when you're done. If you're practicing for ACA tournaments, I recommend buying and training with their official flies made with rooster hackle, then you'll get used to how they cast and appear on different backdrops and under different lighting.

Once you have your outfit and have learned a little about its various parts and components, I'd like to take a second to help you take care of them. Although rod manufacturers have special warranty and replacement policies, it's best to avoid needing to use them. It can take time and it's a disappointment when sections for older rods are obsolete.

The most common way to snap a rod is in a door or trunk. The next most common destroyer of rods is to raise the tip of the rod when fighting a fish and it swims under the angler or boat. This is called high-sticking. When a fish gets too close, raise the rod-butt and point the rod tip down toward the fish to bend the rod more in the stronger butt section. Another way to break a rod is to reach up and bend the tip so you can grab the line. I've also heard horror stories of leaving rods loosely on top of vehicles and remembering miles later. They often end badly.

It's funny, but ACA distance casting participants leave their rods laying on the ground all over the place at events and I've never seen one get stepped on by a caster. It just takes a little awareness of your surroundings.

INSTRUCTION AND DIY

Fly fishing is not a sport that's easy to learn. The most successful way to learn it is through a mentor at an early age. This works best if there is a personal connection between student and teacher. This person might be a family member, a friend, or a professional who takes a personal interest. The best ways to learn to cast are to watch and mimic good casters and to have an

This is the McLaren Lodge of the Golden Gate Angling and Casting Club in Golden Gate Park, San Francisco, CA. Photo: George Mccabe.

instructor or mentor show you the right way and teach good habits. On your own, you might start bad ones.

If you don't have a close fly fishing mentor, you can find instructors and people willing to share their knowledge. Not everyone has access to clubs and instructors, so you may need to use books, videos, and help from friends and family. The important thing is to engage in your passion to fly fish to the best of your ability wherever you can. In order to learn and improve, all you need is your willingness, a bit of tackle, and a lawn, athletic field, or local body of water.

The American Casting Association is good place to watch, get instruction, and practice. The ACA has about sixteen clubs at this printing which offer free lessons and have casting ponds on which to learn and practice. There is a list of locations and contact info later in this book. Casting at targets at set distances gives you a way to judge your own results and something to build upon. Fly Fishers International, which is a conservation and educational organization, has affiliates around the world and individual certified casting instructors available. Independent schools and fly shops also offer group and private instruction.

Visual verification that your body, your rod, and your line are doing what they are supposed to is one of the most important tools in learning to cast well. Seeing what's going on will help identify faults and flaws. Practicing the right way from the beginning will shorten your learning curve. If instead you repeat and practice a defective stroke, correction may take years, even with professional help. If an instructor or experienced friend spots a fault that you do not understand or confirm, have them record it on video for you to see. It's easier to believe and understand faults if you see them yourself.

You can also learn on your own if you don't have regular access to a club or instruction. Even if you do, you should also practice on your own once you get the basics. I recommend learning to cast on an athletic field or a park lawn instead of on the water, except for the roll cast, which I'll explain later. Avoid casting on paving, concrete, sand, or gravel. These will damage your line and the grit is not good for the rest of your outfit either. If possible, record your casting with a tablet or camera on a tripod so you can check your form.

CHAPTER 2

A GOOD FOUNDATION

One thing all good American Casting Association casters share is the way they cast. Some people call this "Western tournament style." It has evolved for the needs of good accuracy and has proven itself on many fine fishing waters. Good casters have good back casts and the ability to make a narrow loop in their fly line during a cast when needed. A narrow loop will travel through the air more easily than a wide one because it is less air resistant and helps with placing a fly more accurately. This, combined with the ability to make the line travel very fast, increases casting distance and helps overcome the negative effects of wind.

In sports that use a racquet, bat, club, or rod, the motion or swing with the hand gripping the handle is called the stroke. A good stroke should be efficient so there is little wasted effort. It should enable you to use your strength and speed to reach the target and help you put the fly in the middle of it. If you learn a good casting stroke you will spend less energy, reduce fatigue,

It's useful to learn how to produce a wide, medium, or narrow loop when the need calls. The narrow loop is the hardest to master.

and achieve better results. In tournament casting this translates to a higher score, whereas in angling it represents catching more fish. Also remember it's easier to learn the right way at first than to go back and fix faults later. First, I'm going to discuss stance, the use of the rod hand making the stroke, then how to control the line with the line hand.

STANCE

Good learning habits start with control and repetition. The foundation in most sports and fly casting, is the stance. To begin learning to cast, stand in a square stance with your hips square to the target and your body facing the casting direction. In this position, your feet should be about shoulder width apart to form a comfortable base. Most people also call this position a closed stance. If you drop one foot back, it's an open stance. An open stance puts the feet on an imaginary line at an angle to the target. When anglers wade in current, they stand sideways with one hip into the flow to decrease drag. When you are on land, a dock, or on a vessel, your stance is not as limited. There is a different stance for distance casting and I'll cover that later.

THE CASTING STROKE

A cast with a fly rod begins when you start the stroke which moves the rod, line, leader and fly. The caster's shoulder, the elbow, and the wrist rotate and the rod tip accelerates the line. The stroke bends the rod against the resistance of the line and this bending and unbending helps maintain tension and increases line speed. To make a controlled loop, stop the rod with your rod hand and the line in the shape of a loop will continue its unrolling flight. Just the top part of the loop unrolls. This unrolling loop cuts through the air to deliver the fly. I'll explain how to vary the size of the loop a little later in this book.

There must be enough line speed transferred to the cast to unroll the end of the fly line and leader. The cast has many times been compared to flicking water from a paintbrush or throwing an apple off a fork. To deliver the fly to the target or water after the loop is formed, lower your rod tip until it nearly touches the water, or grass if you are lawn casting.

There are two strokes, one for the back cast and one for the forward cast. When you first learn casting and you're not casting for distance, the back cast should be aimed upward and the stroke and the fly line must overcome gravity on the way up. The rod hand should move in a downward arc during the forward stroke on short to medium casts. The most natural and efficient casting stroke uses gravity to help the downward movement of the forward stroke and helps the line travel downward and unroll to the intended target. The stroke and the movement of the rod and line, are linked together. The three joints that provide this rotation are the shoulder, elbow and wrist joints.

Proper rotation of the stroke causes rod tip speed which is mostly responsible for the ability to create high line speed in the cast. We need adequate line speed when casting considerable distances and when overcoming wind resistance. Not only does the arm and shoulder provide acceleration but they also stabilize the rod when casting with wind resistance on the line, rod, and body.

If you must repeat hundreds of casts a day on the water or in a tournament, use the largest muscles possible. This applies even in performing the smallest casts. Using the shoulders and core will stabilize the rod plane and reduces the fatigue of smaller muscles. This is why good casters don't rely on the wrist for doing most casting. The wrist is used in conjunction with bigger muscles and large joint rotation. If your shoulder rotates on your forward cast you are using your *latissimus dorsi* muscle to help pull your hand down and bend the rod. If you learn the correct mechanics and timing, these movements combine to make a tight loop and the ability to cast your farthest.

The ability to make an upward back cast is a sign of expertise. A good back cast helps you make a good forward cast. The back cast is usually more difficult than the forward casts for most casters to master. First, you can watch the forward cast easily but watching what's going on behind is more difficult. Secondly, the back cast is more difficult than the forward cast because the muscles available to move the rod back are not as strong as the muscles to move the rod forward.

GRIP

Most of the casters in ACA use one of two grips, either the thumb on top grip, or the v-grip. They are almost identical except for the thumb placement and a slight turn. To use the v-grip, place the handle in your palm on a 45-degree angle so it touches the heel of your palm, and is held between the thumb and index finger with the other fingers wrapped at the first joint. Extend the index finger up the grip slightly as shown. With the thumb on top grip, the thumb should be on top of the handle and in the v-grip; turn your wrist so it's on the side.

Chris Korich, ACA Hall of Famer and "Casting Jedi" of the Oakland Casting Club says the grip should be loose and "slingy," only catching and gripping the handle with light pressure to stop the rod to

The first photo is a closeup of Chris Korich showing the contact points for the "V" or extended-finger grip. The next photo is Chris gripping the handle.

end the stroke. The rod should almost float in your hand and absorb its own vibrations. If you grip too tightly, it tends to amplify them. The first thing to do is relax your body since muscle tension prevents fluid joint movements.

ROD PLANE

For short and medium casts, stopping the hand near the face helps your aim. It's like throwing darts. When you are making a cast, you should tilt the rod a little to the side and outside the body so the fly and line don't strike you or the rod. You can do this by bending your wrist or elbow joint a little outward. There will be times when fishing when you might want to tilt the rod a lot for various reasons I'll cover later. Always wear glasses to protect your eyes when casting.

Once you've established the rod angle to use, make sure you cast with your rod in one plane from the beginning of your stroke to the end. This will let the loop form and unroll without twisting and failing. How straight your rod travels in this plane is called tracking. If I see a caster's hand rotate incorrectly, causing the rod tip to curve inward or outward, I'd call it a tracking error.

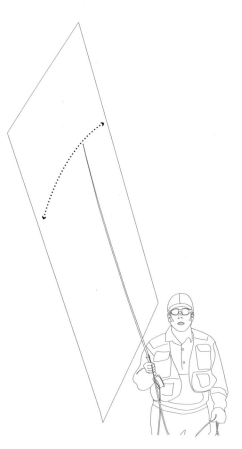

While you are performing overhead casts, the rod should be constrained to travel in one plane to produce an efficient loop.

ROD STOP

To make a loop that is usable in a fishing or tournament situation, you must stop the rod with the rod hand. If you don't, the resulting loop will be extremely wide and virtually uncontrollable. To make a decent loop, you want to make the stop quickly. The line should have a minimum of little waves up and down its length. Shocking the rod by bouncing it when you make a stop can cause such waves. We like to call a good stop a soft stop. The time and distance it takes you to stop the rod can affect the arc. The more protracted the stop, the more rod rotates and too much opens the loop. Think of the stop like the brakes in a car. If you have brake fade it's not good. You might have an accident. If your brakes stop quickly, you might avoid one.

ROD ARC AND THE LOOP

There are only a few terms of casting jargon in this beginner's book but they will help you shorten your learning curve if you learn them. I ask your forgiveness in advance. Rod arc is the change in angle of the rod's lower section from one stop in your cast to the next. The amount of rod arc has the most effect of the size of the loop. If your rod hand rotates less, the rod will rotate less. If the rod rotates less, the loop will be smaller; but if your hand and the rod rotate more, the loop will be bigger. Your rod hand can rotate from the wrist, elbow, and shoulder. If a cast has insufficient rod arc, it will cause a tailing loop.

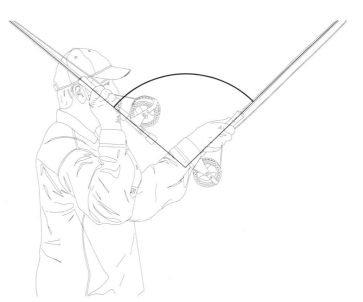

This drawing of rod-arc shows the measurable angle the rod butt has traveled during a cast.

FALSE CASTS

If you lay the fly down and on the water or grass at the end of a cast, you have presented the fly with what we call a delivery, or a lay-down. If you make a series of casts without laying the fly down, they are called false casts. You would make false casts when aiming, adjusting cast length, or drying a dry fly in the air. False casting is also done for other reasons I'll explain later.

180-DEGREE PRINCIPLE

The 180-degree principle states that the angle of the back cast and the forward cast must be directly opposite each other. This is in order for the rod tip to pull the line in the most direct efficient line and produce a good loop. Think of casting at imaginary targets located in 180-degree opposite directions with a line connecting them.

The angle of the rod when you make your forward and back cast stops will determine where the casts go. The amount of rod arc and stroke length between the stops has to be correct for the amount of line cast, or loop mistakes will arise. For example, if I make a low back cast and a low forward cast, it would produce a wide inefficient loop. If you were to make a high

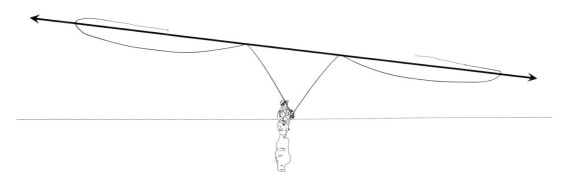

The 180-degree principle: Back cast and forward casts should be directly opposite in order to form a good loop.

This photo shows a tailing loop. It is a casting fault and usually ruins the cast. Photo: Edina Field.

back cast and a high forward cast, it would result in a tailing loop. You can identify a tailing loop when the line from the fly to the front of the loop cross below the line from the point of the loop to the rod and there is an upward curve in the line and leader past this intersection. In the worst tailing loop, the fly leg also crosses the rod leg of the loop twice and resembles a figure eight on its side, as in the accompanying photo.

TRAJECTORY

The trajectory of a cast is the angle of the cast in relation to horizontal, or what we think of as bubble level. The trajectory can be on an upward or downward angle. One of the first considerations when picking trajectory for a cast is clearing objects and snags on our back cast.

Ideally, the energy of a cast should transfer down the line and open the loop and leader just before the fly reaches the target. Estimating cast trajectory should include the anticipated effect of gravity, wind carry, or wind resistance. Gravity will also have a greater negative affect on casts in an upward angle compared to those made "downhill." We aim our casts 180 degrees apart to direct the energy of the next cast toward our next target. For example, a low forward cast requires a high back cast.

If an angler casts toward a specific target, the caster needs to compensate for any elevation difference between the caster and the target. If the caster is on a boat or jetty, the angle will be greater to a given target than if wading. We establish the angle of the back cast to avoid objects, and on a forward delivery, to reach our intended target, whether they are at twenty feet or a hundred feet.

It pays to use a higher back cast when casting a heavy fly or high-density line. These heavier or less air resistant objects will fall faster in air than a bulkier floating line of the same line weight with a light fly due to aerodynamics. A caster can use trajectory in her favor in windy conditions. This will be covered in the distance chapter.

TIMING AND TEMPO

The back cast is the setup for the forward cast, so it is especially important to eliminate slack in the back cast. Slack wastes the stroke and prevents efficiency. Good timing helps reduce slack on the back cast. Timing in fly casting refers to the pause waiting for a loop to unroll in the air and the moment a cast is started in a different direction. During this time gravity is acting on your line leader and fly in varying degrees. Pausing too little as well as pausing too long causes problems.

When you make a back cast and a forward cast in succession, you should pause for the line to unroll on the back cast, then make the next cast. Gravity will cause a little sagging in the middle where most of the weight is but that's normal. It is not necessary to see the leader straighten completely since it has less weight.

If your pause is too short and you start your forward cast too early while the loop is still unrolling backward, the momentum will force the loop open, causing it to make a cracking sound like a whip. This wastes energy and the rod is not pulling on the whole weight of the extended line, and some of the line is essentially dead weight. You can only cast the portion of the line that is relatively straight or under tension. This will not make an efficient forward cast.

If you pause too long, the line will fall too much, causing slack and misalignment from your intended trajectory. The cast is not acting upon the weight of the slack portion of the line. This lack of energy and deformity in the line will produce an inefficient cast with poor turnover. Also, if you aim your back cast too low and you wait too long, the fly might "tick" on the back cast, which scares fish, causes slack, and if it hits a rock, it can ruin your hook.

The pace at which you make casts back and forth is the tempo of your casts. Think of your rod as the hand of a metronome making even movements interspersed with pauses for the line to straighten. Assuming there is no wind, and you're not casting far, false casts should be made with a slow tempo. This will also increase the need to pause longer than on a fast-paced cast of the same length.

It's best to use only as much line speed as necessary to make a cast with good tension and smoothness. A slow tempo is best for short casts, since the amount of line extended is short and gravity won't have much of an affect. This is also a necessary discipline for short-range presentations to spooky fish. The slower and softer a fly line, leader, and fly land on the water, the less commotion they will make.

There are times when a fast tempo is needed. A fast tempo is needed to keep long casts aloft because of the additional line weight and time in the air. Increasing tempo can help reduce line sag due to gravity and effects of wind drift as well.

GOING THROUGH THE MOTIONS

Sometimes learning to do something without distractions can help your muscle memory learn it faster than trying to keep several things going at once. Practicing a casting stroke without a line or without even a fly outfit eliminates thinking of timing or other things at the same time.

Chris Korich asked a large group of students signed up for a group casting lesson at the Long Beach Casting Club to come with their rod butt (lower) section and their reels but didn't share why. When they came, he had them line up and practice the foundation stroke before doing any casting. Take the lower section of your rod with the reel on and do the following casts in slow motion anywhere or in front of a mirror so you can see what you're doing. When you can do them automatically, do them at normal speed.

Make a back cast starting with a straight wrist and the rod away from you in a 45-degree position. We'll call this the bottom position. Your upper arm should be straight up and down and the lower arm should be almost horizontal. Your elbow should be close to your side and your entire body should be relaxed.

To start the cast, lift your rod hand by closing your elbow joint and rotating your wrist backward all the way through the stroke. Lift the elbow about two inches simultaneously during the back cast and the shoulder will have to rotate. When the rod is at about the one o'clock position behind, stop the stroke with a soft stop. There should now be a space of about three inches between the rod butt and your forearm. I use three fingers together to gauge this space.

Using pantomime can help you learn in steps more easily. The author is pantomiming the bottom position of a cast. This is the beginning point of a back cast and the stopping point for a forward cast. Photo: Edina Field.

The author is pantomiming the bottom position of a cast. This is the stopping point of a back cast and the beginning point for a forward cast. Photo: Edina Field.

This photo shows the bottom position with a rod in hand. Use the bottom and top position still photos and descriptions to help you set up your arm to learn this stroke. Photo: Edina Field.

This photo shows the top position with a rod in hand. Photo: Edina Field.

Your casting hand should stop at about eye height. The forearm should be almost upright. Pause now on the back cast and wait for unrolling loop behind. We'll call this the top position.

Next, let's break down the forward cast. When the line is almost completely unrolled on the back cast, and before it starts falling, start the forward cast by doing next three things at the same time. Rotate the rod hand downward by straightening your wrist. Open your elbow and rotate your shoulder until the upper arm is straight up and down. Stop the stroke affirmatively when the rod is approximately at a 45-degree angle.

Time your wrist rotation so it straightens at the same point as your stop. Your upper arm joint should rotate backward at the shoulder and the elbow should fall during the forward cast. This movement will insure that the *latissimus dorsi* muscle will work as if pulling on an oar. The arm should be at the bottom position once again. You can also pantomime this drill without a rod and use the same anatomical references.

LINE CONTROL

When you present a fly to a fish, too much slack between the rod tip and a fish or between the stripper guide and your line hand is bad. It can cause you to lose fish on the strike. It is also harder to make a pick up to cast when there is slack. A straight line is easier to lift into the air than a wiggly line with slack in it. Usually it's wise to only have enough line off the reel that you will cast or it can tangle or get caught on something. The simplest way to control slack is to keep the rod tip as low as possible before casting and to always strip-in slack.

The main function of the line hand in casting is to control slack and either lengthen the line fed into a cast or to strip it in to shorten the cast. In order to cast you must hold the line by either pinching the line against the handle with your index finger or holding it in your line hand. Move the line hand (with the line) in unison with the casting hand when false-casting and your line hand will be trained to stay in the proper relationship.

The rod hand does the indispensable task of casting and the line hand controls the line for casting, stripping, or playing a fish. When you're stripping-in line with the line hand, the rod hand plays a small but essential role too.

You can place the line under the index finger on the rod hand and either let the line slide through, or stop and hold it with finger pressure. You alternately slip and hold when making length changes and when you're making a strip-retrieve when fishing with flies like a streamer. Stopping the line in this manner holds it while your line hand slides up the line for the next strip. Otherwise, there would be no resistance if a fish struck the fly at that instant. You might lose the fish or get tangled.

There is seldom a time when you actually let go of the fly line. One is when you shoot line without letting it run through your hand, or when you're playing a fish on the reel.

In the next chapter we will learn about cast basics while practicing the mechanics just covered. How to combine these into fishing presentations will come later.

CHAPTER 3

CAST BASICS

Learning to coordinate the rod hand and line hand in basic casts with good timing will enable you to move toward casting proficiency. ACA casters learn basic casts and techniques in accuracy events and are the foundation for learning maximum distance and specialized fishing casts and presentations. I will provide some fun drills to help make these casts more automatic for you. The roll cast and the pick-up and lay-down are the two most important casts to learn.

ROLL CAST

The first cast I'd like a beginner to start is the roll cast because of its simplicity and usefulness. The main use of a roll cast is to replace a cast overhead when you don't have enough room behind to make a proper back cast. You can also make a roll cast to straighten out slack line beyond the rod tip.

There are four parts to making a roll cast: D-loop, pause, forward cast, and lay-down. To begin a roll cast, you slowly drag a loop of line behind the rod tip in the shape of the letter "D" which partially hangs in the air and partially lies on the water. We call this the D-loop. The part that that lies in the water has water tension exerted on it and we call that portion the "anchor." Because the D-loop is slack, the line has insufficient weight, and it needs resistance in order for the rod to accelerate the line. The anchor and the weight of the hanging loop provide it. The D-loop takes the place of a back cast.

This cast can be learned on the grass but I recommend learning it on water so you can feel water tension on the line and use it to make the cast. Water tension holds the end of the line

The author is using a Z-mend to wiggle line out though the guides in a hurry to perform a roll cast. Photo: Edina Field.

then releases it as you pick it up of the water. You can simulate this effect by using a clipboard and holding the leader in the clip. You can also have a friend hold the leader underfoot and release it when the cast is made. A roll cast is easier with a floating line, since the line is left on the water for an instant, whereas a sinking line would sink, making the cast more difficult—but not impossible—to lift.

To get line on the water for a roll cast if you haven't put any out by other means, use the Z-Mend. It is a quick way and is commonly used in the roll cast round of the ACA Trout Fly Accuracy event. Strip out the measured amount of line needed to make the cast—let's say about twenty-five feet of line, plus the leader. Elevate the reel until the rod tip is almost in the water and wiggle the rod tip from side to side to stack-mend line in the water. You regulate the slipping line with the line hand and the water tension anchors the line so each rod movement lays out more line. You can also submerge the tip and snap gently up to pull more line out of the rod tip.

To make the D-loop, have your rod tip pointed down toward the water and slowly lift the rod so the line starts to break free from the water and feeling the water tension, slide the line backward with your rod tip away from your body on your casting side. Don't stop until the rod tip is at about the one o'clock position behind you and the back part of line forms the D-loop hanging behind the rod tip. Check and adjust the angle of the rod if necessary, so the rod tip, D-loop, and fly are in a line 180 degrees opposite the target. If the D-loop hits you in the back, make sure you aren't turning your hand inward when you make your alignment, before making the cast.

The butt and leader connection of your line should be alongside you but not behind, otherwise the anchor can slip and prevent the required resistance to make the cast. When everything is aligned and your rod hand is on the same level as your ear, pause for a split second to aim, then make the forward stroke ending in a stop, then follow the line to the water to make a lay-down. Use the same forward-stroke mechanics I described in the last chapter.

When setting up a roll cast with line already on the water, but not aligned with your next target, align the rod tip, D-loop, and fly by sliding them with your rod tip across the water. If your fly line, leader, and fly line up in front of you or on your wrong

Proper alignment of the D-loop, fly, and target to make a good safe roll cast. Photo: Edina Field.

side, attempt to move yourself left or right until they are safely on your casting side. If your line, leader, and fly cannot be slid into safe alignment on your casting side, change the side of your body you make the cast by using an Off-Shoulder roll cast. This puts the path of the line and fly safely beyond the opposite shoulder. You don't need to be hit or have a crossed loop or tangle. Another reason to use an Off-Shoulder roll cast instead of a regular roll cast would be if there is a wind on your casting side. Safety first.

Make the Off-Shoulder roll cast by lifting the elbow of your casting arm and tilt the rod over your head so the rod tip is now beyond the opposite shoulder. Stop the rod with your hand a few inches away from the top of your head. Hold the line with your line hand and move it outward so the line is not in your face. You will be looking through the opening between the line and the rod as if you were looking through

The author is showing proper D-loop, fly, and target alignment while making an Off-Shoulder roll cast. Photo: Edina Field.

a window. You can get extra angle for the long casts by reaching your casting hand backward over your head to stop the rod.

If you need to make a very short roll cast but it doesn't seem you have enough line to achieve an anchor or form a D-loop, try kneeling or squatting, so more line lies on the water. If on the other hand you need to make a long cast, you'll need to tighten the loop and speed things up. If you start your roll cast stroke too briskly without continued acceleration, it will throw the line in circle and the loop will be round and wide. If you start your forward stroke slowly with your wrist cocked open and accelerate continuously until the stop, most of the energy will be narrowly focused and the loop should be tighter.

There are also three techniques you can use in conjunction with a tight loop to increase distance. The first is to move as much of the D-loop behind you as possible. You do this by slowly lifting almost all the line off the water and jump it to the anchor point so the line leader connection is about a rod's length away and then pause. Throwing the D-loop backward is only possible if you have enough room behind you. Lift as much of the line off the water as possible by raising your rod tip and make the forward cast.

The second technique is to use a side-arm stroke and bring the rod tip back and away from the casting shoulder. This set-up also maximizes the length of line in the D-loop with which to accelerate the line and increases stroke length. Before making the cast, lift the D-loop off the water with the rod tip to reduce the length of line adhering to the water from water tension and causing resistance to your lift. Then, accelerate into the cast and end with a positive stop.

Third, is to start with your weight on your back foot and then move your weight forward into the cast like you're throwing a ball. Joan Wulff, champion caster and Wulff School of Fly Fishing instructor, is adamant about using the body in the roll cast. Remember to observe the 180-Degree Principle with your rod tip, D-loop, and anchor aligned.

Joan Salvato Wulff is a champion caster, author, and instructor of the Wulff School of Fly Fishing. This is a photo of Joan in 1965 at a sportsman's show. Photo: Bob Howard.

PICK-UP AND LAY-DOWN

Once you've learned how to roll cast, you'll have learned the basic forward cast that you can use in the pick-up and lay-down. In the roll-cast, the D-loop is the setup for the forward cast, but in an overhead cast, the setup is a fully extended back cast. The Pick-up and Lay-down are the two halves in performing one overhead casting cycle, as opposed to a roll cast.

The pick-up and lay-down has five parts; pick-up, back cast, pause, forward cast, and lay-down. The pick-up begins with the length of line you want to cast outstretched in front of you. Let's start with thirty feet plus the leader. You can strip and wiggle it out and use a roll cast to get the line into this position and follow it to the water with the rod tip. Make sure there is no slack beyond the tip by stripping in a loop and letting it hang from the reel. You should have about twenty-five feet of line plus the leader past the rod tip. Pinch the line to the handle with the index finger of your rod hand. Your forearm will be approximately horizontal.

Next, start the pick-up by slowly lifting the line off the ground or water by rotating your arm and shoulder. Continue into a back cast moving through the bottom position up to the top position on the back cast. Stop the rod with your rod hand and pause with the rod at about the one o'clock position for a fast one count. During the pause, you want the loop made by the back cast to unroll without falling. Now start the forward cast. End the forward cast by positively stopping the rod about forty-five degrees over the water, then immediately lower the rod tip down to follow the line down to the water to make the lay-down. If you don't make a lay-down, the line will be taut off your rod tip and slack will be produced when you eventually lower the rod. This slack will rob you of control and the ability to hook fish.

FALSE CAST

A false cast is a cast in either the back-cast direction or forward-cast direction, which you do not intentionally place on the water or land. A false cast is a good way to dry a dry fly or to estimate target distance for proper line length. You can also shorten or lengthen the line while doing it. You can also make a change of casting direction by moving your aiming points toward your new target in increments. You may follow any number of false casts with a lay-down, as with the pick-up and lay-down drill.

FALSE CAST DRILL

- Start with sets of thirty-foot false casts and lay the fly down after each set.
- Start your stroke with your rod tip near the ground and with no slack in fly line.
- Use only enough grip pressure to control and stop the rod.
- Cast without moving your body.
- Your hand should reach the height of your ear on the back cast.
- Aim your forward cast low and your back cast high.
- Make both strokes with the same speed (assuming no opposing wind).
- Cast smoothly and softly and during the pause do not wait so long that the line falls.
- After the lay-down, follow the line down with your rod tip until the tip is just off the ground and there is no slack. If there is slack, strip in slack until line is tight.
- Observe the loops in the air and see if they are tailing or crossing over, or if the loops are too wide.
- Make any necessary adjustments on several repetitive sets of casts. If you cannot cure faults, do not continue. Please refer to the Trouble-Shooting chapter.
- If your loops look beautiful, increase cast length by a few feet and reexamine your loops.

During false casts in either direction, do not drop the rod tip or open your grip after the stop. At this moment, the loop is forming or unrolling and this would open the loop. Once the loop is formed beyond the rod tip on your lay-down cast and the line is falling, follow the line downward with your rod tip.

LENGTHENING AND SHORTENING LINE (WITHOUT HAULING)

Adjustments in cast length require good line handling to maintain control and prevent tangles. Shooting or slipping line can be performed either on the back cast, forward cast, or both. Shooting is when the line hand releases line immediately after the rod stop and the cast pulls line out through the guides. Slipping line is when you release your hold on the line with the fingers of your line hand and let line slip under control through your hand to extend the length of your cast, then pinch the line again with your fingers to stop it. You will often slip line to help adjust the correct distance to make a false, or presentation cast.

When aiming a cast at a given target, you have to get both the cast length and direction correct. The way to do this with the most control is to false cast with the line pinned against the handle with the index finger of the casting hand. You can shorten the cast by stripping line back through the index finger with the line hand. To extend the cast, you can loosen the index finger and let small amounts slip through, until the length is right. Or, you can release the line from that index finger and make adjustments with the line hand. I like to slip and adjust length with the line hand.

When trying to extend a cast as far as possible without hauling, you can let the line shoot through your fingers or release the line completely from the line hand. If you need to stop it at an exact spot, letting it run through your fingers lets you stop it precisely. If you're blind casting or distance casting, letting go is better, since it reduces friction.

Here are a few drills to help learn how to achieve good line control and getting your casts to the right length.

1. Lengthening drill: 25 feet, 30 feet, 35 feet (ten repetitions); Off-Shoulder drill 25 feet, 30 feet, 35 feet (ten repetitions)
2. Shortening drill: 25 feet, 30 feet, 35 feet (ten repetitions); Off-Shoulder drill 25 feet, 30 feet, 35 feet (ten repetitions)
3. Shooting drill: Diagonal targets limited to two false casts

HAULING LINE: SINGLE AND DOUBLE

A haul is a precisely-timed tug on the line below the stripper guide for the main purpose of adding speed to the line. In addition, it can be used to increase tension on the fly line and eliminate slack, which increases efficiency. Hauling increases casting distance and helps combat wind. Hauling the line in conjunction with good rod speed will accelerate the line faster than the rod hand alone. Double-hauling shares the work between both of your hands and makes false casting easier in conditions where you have more line out. If you can already make nice loops, hauling should make them a little tighter, if done correctly.

A single-haul is a single pull and return move on either the forward or back cast, but not both. The first motion is down, the second

The arrows in this drawing indicate that the execution of the haul should mirror the timing start and finish of the stroke.

is up. Tournament champion Steve Rajeff likes to teach the haul by saying, "bounce" when the line hand stops and the haul changes directions. Generally, hauls should mirror the timing of the rod hand. When the rod hand is moving, the line hand should be moving. The acceleration of a fly line should be steady. Increase the speed of the haul smoothly from start to finish.

The return move is a repositioning of the line hand toward the stripper guide so it is ready to strip, haul again, or set the hook if needed. You make the return after the stop during the pause. The momentum of the cast pulls the line up through the guides. To prevent slack, the rate you return the hauled line should match the line's pull upward though the guides. You can single-haul on either a forward cast or back cast. You might false cast using a single-haul only into the wind or for a pick-up. In both the single and the double-haul, you have the option of casting a fixed length of line or shooting more into the cast. You may also use a single-haul to increase the distance of a roll-cast. I have a drill to learn hauls using the same layout as the horizontal casting drill.

The first will help teach you do a single-haul. Start with about twenty feet of line and the leader out beyond the rod tip and cast it down the line toward an end cone. Drag any slack tight and with your rod pointing at the end cone, grab the line half way between the reel and the stripper guide. Make a low cast toward the other end cone. As you cast, haul and return the line before the line lands. Let the line and fly land and take a look at your work. The fly line should be extended and your hauling hand that returned the line should be in the same half-way position. Now cast, haul and return in the other direction. You should move your rod so it is approximately 45 degrees to your left and to your right when you stop and pause on each cast. Once you can perform these single hauls, you will be ready to move on to the double-haul.

The double-haul is performed on a minimum of two consecutive casts and ends in either returning line and holding it, or shooting it into the cast. The return not only repositions the line hand for the following haul but returns a length of line into the cast equal to the length of the next haul. If you hauled down during a false cast, you would end with your line hand extended, unable to repeat the haul.

The length of the haul should correspond to the length of the cast being made: the longer the cast, the longer the haul; the shorter the cast, the shorter the haul should be. This will help prevent making too long of a haul and creating slack. The hauling speed should also be proportional to the speed used in the rod stroke.

When hauling or holding line in the line hand, pinch the line between the thumb, index and optionally, the middle finger. The fewer fingers involved, the easier it will be to release the line cleanly. If you hold onto the line too long after the stop before you release, it will open the size of the loop. You can haul, shoot, and recapture the line in the line hand repetitively in a shooting and hauling sequence.

Now that you've read about the double-haul and can perform a single-haul, it's time to do a drill for the double-haul that picks up where the single left off. Instead of letting the cast land while single-hauling, make false casts without them touching the ground, then add double-hauls in the following manner. Haul during the strokes and return line during the pauses.

Start a double-haul with a tug on the line at the beginning of the stroke and, without letting go of the line at the stop, return line up through the guides during the pause. The angle at which you haul should be down, forward, and slightly away from the reel, or line can wrap on both the reel and rod butt. Try visualizing the movement of the hands doing a double-haul as: hands apart, hands together, or the line hand goes down, and up.

The length of the hauls on a back cast or forward cast should be of equal lengths when making casts of equal distance without a head or tail wind. Uneven hauls nullify line speed and casting potential. The haul made on the delivery should longer than the preceding false cast when the delivery is longer than the preceding cast. This is the case when you shoot line on the delivery.

DOUBLE-HAUL FALSE CAST DRILL

If you've done the horizontal hauling drill, you've experienced the timing and feeling of it. I'd like you to leave the cones and next try doing several nice slow false casts overhead with the rod slightly angled away from your body with twenty-five feet of line out plus the leader. Now add double-hauls. Remember to make your hauls short for a short cast and not too fast, since this is a slow, controlled exercise. If your hauling hand returns quickly after the bounce, there shouldn't be slack.

SHOOTING LINE WITH HAULS

You've practiced accelerating the line with single and double hauls and that should enable you to carry extra line length in the air and reduce slack, but that is only part of the way to a long cast. To really let it fly, you'll have to learn to shoot line after a generous haul and controlled rod stop. If you release the line from the line hand at the stop, it will shoot available line through the rod tip and into the cast. You may shoot line into a forward cast, a back cast, or both, to extend and carry line. How much and when will depend on the circumstances and wind. Try shooting some line until you get the feel and can control the line.

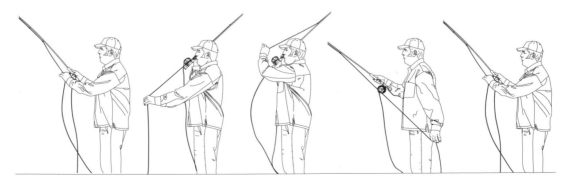

The figure on left is in position to start a cast and the next four are performing the four steps of the double-haul while making back-and-forward false casts.

First try shooting line on your forward cast. When your hauling hand is at the bottom of the haul stroke it should coincide with the rod stop. Release the line from your fingers and let it slide through an "O" formed with the tips of your index finger and thumb. Practice letting the cast land without stopping the line and also try stopping it at different distances to simulate actual circumstances. You could get even more practice doing this to targets at thirty, forty, and fifty feet.

Shooting and extending line on the forward false cast is the next skill to learn to help make fast, long casts. Instead of making a lay-down with the line you shoot, stop it by closing the "O" and recapture it between your index and thumb as soon as it straightens, then continue making your back cast. As you increase the length of the line you carry, increase the length of your stroke and haul.

Next, attempt shooting line on your back cast and make some lay-downs. After you can present with your back cast and shoot line, start false casting with a short line and shoot and extend the length of your casts by shooting and recapturing the line like you did above. Minimizing the number of false casts saves time and motion. This is the way to get the line out to make a cast to a fish as fast as possible while the opportunity still exists. Sometimes it's only seconds. In Chapter 6: Fishing Casts, I describe the Saltwater Quick Cast (page 70) which details the way to cast while sight fishing in saltwater and large freshwater bodies.

WIND CASTS

Sometimes you can't choose the weather you fish in, like when you book a guide in advance and have to take what nature brings each day. In some situations, it's good to have some wind to trigger predatory behavior in the fish or to have the waves disguise your presence. The biggest downside when trying to fish in windy conditions is getting enough casting distance. Seeing fish and not being able to reach them is demoralizing when you know you could put it right in front of them if it wasn't blowing so hard. The other problem is putting the fly where you want it without the wind blowing the line off course to the left or right.

The most important thing to do to deal with the effects of wind is to increase the line speed of your casts. The way to do that is through faster stroke pace, a narrow loop, maximized double-haul technique, and effective body movement, which I'll cover in the distance chapter. There are, however, avoidances and special casts which have evolved to mitigate the effects of the wind.

Remember, wind is seldom constant, so use any break between gusts or favorable change in wind angle, to make a better cast. When possible, reposition and change your casting angle if the wind is on your casting side so you are either casting directly downwind, or quartering downwind on your line hand side. Remember everyone's safety is your first priority. That doesn't, however, address what the wind will do when you have your back cast into it. Even if you can make tight loops with fast line speed, you have some options for the best cast to use for windy conditions.

This is a low side-arm cast, which can be used to defeat wind or to cast under overhanging branches or docks. Photo: Edina Field.

If the wind is blowing onto the same side as your line hand, it's not much of a problem. It will probably suffice to use additional line speed to prevent wind drift on your line and fly to maintain distance and accuracy. If the wind is blowing into your casting shoulder, it is a potential hazard because the fly and line can hit you. If you can choose which side of a river to stand on, or reposition yourself in a boat, or when wading, it can help you avoid the danger.

If the wind is light, maybe five miles per hour, additional line speed will help. When fishing in a light breeze, I recommend a low side-arm stroke. This will separate you and the hook by almost a rod length. Make sure you increase line speed so it doesn't hit the water during false casts. When it's blowing ten to fifteen miles per hour, I recommend the Off-Shoulder cast.

To make the right-handed Off-Shoulder cast, angle the casting plane overhead so the rod tip is over the shoulder of the line hand. You do this by lifting the elbow of your casting arm, with the casting hand stopping above the right ear. This places the rod tip and path of the line and fly downwind, out past the other shoulder. Move the line hand outward so the line is not in your face. You will be looking through the opening between the line and the rod as if looking through a window.

If there is a good wind blowing on your casting side, I recommend the Barnegat Bay cast for safety and comfort. I thought I'd cite the name of this cast because of the saltwater fly-fishing history of the New Jersey shore. When right-handed casters are casting to the East in this stretch of water, the prevailing stiff breeze from the South blows dangerously into their casting side. The local fly rodders learned long ago to turn their backs to the wind and deliver the presentation with their back casts. Thus, the name of the cast which is now used by fly casters worldwide, to let the wind blow the line and fly away from, instead of into them.

In the cases when you are casting downwind or forced to cast against the wind, you have to control your line speed to match to take advantage of it. False casting with the wind can cause excessive line speed with a loss of control, resulting in a bullwhip effect. It should be done with reduced stroke and hauling effort to prevent problems. Shooting too much line with the wind while false casting can cause problems on the next cast since it's into the wind.

When you're casting with a tailwind, or downwind, and the wind is at your back, the wind will help carry your forward cast, but unfortunately the wind will also put the brakes on your back cast. Don't shoot too much line into the wind on the back cast or the loop might not turn over. It's more effective to shoot more line downwind on the presentation. Angle your back cast downward to reduce lift and angle the forward cast correspondingly upward. The wind will help carry and open the forward cast.

When making an off-shoulder cast, move the line away from your face to prevent the line from obstructing your vision. It's like looking through a windowpane. Photo: Edina Field.

If you're casting into a headwind, direct your forward cast as close to the water as possible and direct your back cast on an upward trajectory and 180 degrees away from the forward cast. Presenting close to the surface prevents excessive wind drift. In addition, when casting against the wind, use adequate line speed by making a harder stroke and or a faster double-haul. A headwind will have an effect on back cast timing because loops open faster down wind, but may stay aloft longer due to wind drag. Remember, shooting line downwind into a back cast might over-bend when you make your forward cast into the wind. This will cause a wide loop and lost line speed.

When the wind is howling and you're wading in the open, try using very low sidearm casts with a downwind delivery. By casting as close to the water as possible without touching it with the fly or line, you take advantage of three things. First, by reducing the downwards casting angle, you are reducing the frontal area of the line. Secondly, the wind will assist in loop and leader turnover downwind. Even if you don't get good back cast turnover, the force of the wind will straighten that forward cast right out! And lastly, the sidearm position almost assures the fly will not snag you. If given a choice, I'd always take a downwind presentation. If the wind is blowing downstream in running water, consider a downstream presentation. If it's blowing upstream, consider an upstream presentation. This will help with distance and turnover.

Chris Korich uses a lay-down in ACA fly accuracy that helps on windy days. The way to do it is to make a high-speed, tight-looped cast and then lower your rod tip after you release the cast. Chris says it's as though the anchored line is a railroad track to the target. The loop looks like the outline of a boat hull, and in Montana it's called the Madison Cast after the Madison River, where it's useful in its notorious winds. Once the line touches down, the wind has no effect over the portion of the line in the water and the energy transfer down the line until it straightens. This cast and its saltwater equivalent, called the Mulson Wind Cast, are particularly useful for countering side winds. Practice these casts under actual wind conditions at home before testing them on the water.

KIDS

Chris Korich has trained some highly successful adult casters and a few years ago took on the challenge of mentoring an exceptional youngster. He found it taught him some new things and has really enjoyed their student-coach relationship. His student's name is Maxine McCormick and in an unprecedented fashion she has been setting ACA accuracy and distance records in her divisions since she was about nine years old. She and her family also enjoy fly fishing together. She has beaten plenty of adults too, beginning when she was very young. She has learned flawless technique and had the passion to train and compete with great concentration. At the time of this printing she is fourteen years old, stands at five feet, six inches, and is a formidable opponent.

Chris believes learning to cast to targets, as do many instructors including Joan Wulff, is essential in learning to cast well. Chris says the equipment a kid starts out with is number one in importance to learn quickly and enjoy it. The tackle must be proportional to the size and strength of the young caster. It should be easier to cast, slower action (or more bendy), and more fun to keep them interested. All other sports have kid-sized equipment. Chris said, "Like a lightweight whiffle ball and bat. Why give a kid a full sized thirty-inch Ted Williams baseball bat instead?" Tackle manufacturers are just beginning to offer youth-sized rods. Slower action rods like some Fiberglass rods or slower graphite give the rods more feel when casting and are more forgiving of timing errors. He suggests starting eight-to nine-year-olds with shorter, softer rods with smaller-sized handles and a lighter reel to balance the outfit. Chris recently liked the Temple Fork Outfitters Bug Launcher rod, which sells for about $89 US. Echo also has a kids' outfit called the Echo Gecko. Since this rod has a second lower handle section, it can be used two-handed by even some precocious five-year-olds.

Chris thinks skill advancement should be done progressively by building success at short distances and then progressively to farther targets or distances. Pick-ups and lay-downs and false casting are the beginner's most important drills.

Lastly, it must be fun. Intersperse serious practice with breaks. If you don't take breaks, good intensity and willing participation is impossible.

Chris recommends only giving positive reinforcement to kids. Let self-reward eliminate errors. Ignore bad strokes. Tim Rajeff made the same suggestion when I interviewed him about teaching kids. Chris lets his student be aware he is paying attention. Chris suggests taking a personal interest in the everyday life of the student. When Chris is at a tournament, he asks his student to remember the good feelings from making good casts and to repeat those casts as often as possible.

Chris asked Maxine to be aware of the specific link between her muscles and how they enabled her to cast. Chris pointed out Maxine's forearm tendons and muscles that work the wrist and said they were like rubber bands. He asked her to make fun terms for these parts so they could secretly refer to them at an event. Maxine who liked wearing Rainbow Loom bracelets renamed her wrist muscles her Rainbow bands. This was their new code words to use her wrist more. She also named the muscle in shoulder, the "beast muscle." Instead of Chris saying, "make a high back cast," he said, "poke the giant (looking over your shoulder) in the eye with your rod tip!"

When Chris first started training Maxine, they concentrated on the basics and accuracy. When Maxine started to compete, he started training her in thirty-minute sessions, focusing on specific parts of a cast or trying to build on consecutive hits on target in a row. In between sessions Chris would let Maxine take a break. She liked to climb trees and listen to music on her iPod. Breaks are important. When regrouping after an event, he asks her what weaknesses she thinks should be worked on. Good communication and a good relationship is important.

When Chris was a teenager and lived near the Golden Gate Casting and Angling Club, he and his friends Tim and Steve Rajeff received mentoring lessons early by older champion casters. They did well and had the passion to excel and practice. Afternoons after school Chris and Steve would seriously compete against each other, then Tim would join them later for some more relaxed fun like pizza and casting into darkness. When Tim was bored he would change the rules of the casting games and cast with half a rod, wrist only, arm only, different grips and casting angles for fun, but the experimentation helped, he said, to learn versatility and different styles, as well as to expand abilities by switching things up.

The teens played "Hit 'n' Run" in which they had teams and the object was to hit ten targets in a row. On breaks they'd walk to the neighboring polo field and kick field goals. Chris's favorite casting game was ACA's Wet Fly Accuracy which provides lots of repetitions of the pick-up and lay-down with no false casts. You can only estimate and strip line out to shoot into each cast. It helps perfect the back cast since you only get one chance. Chris would set a goal of five perfect rounds before he'd go home. He often practiced in darkness. They'd also compete using all the rods for the other fly accuracy events to increase the challenge.

If you want your kids to get into fishing early before they find out what an iPad is, it's best to start them at about age six or seven with a push button reel and make sure they have a good experience in nature and catch fish. You can upgrade them to spinning tackle a year later and even to fly outfits around age eight or nine. There are some ways to make learning fly casting easier and more fun.

When I start a youngster with a fly rod, I don't give them much instruction at first. I might make a couple short casts so they can try and mimic. I don't even tell them how to hold the rod. Some kids who aren't very strong will take the rod and hold it with two hands. That's ok. I want them to feel the rod bend and see what that does to the line in the air. I encourage discovery because that helps them experience and learn.

Joan Wulff suggests kids draw shapes in the air with the rod tip of a fly rod with about twenty feet of line out. She likes them to makes "circles,

The photo is Maxine McCormick at age twelve at a Trout Unlimited fundraiser in San Francisco. This young lady has achieved worldwide acclaim for her tournament wins and casting records. Photo: Chris Korich.

eights, and straights." This will help them discover what's needed to make a real cast later. Another thing you can do to encourage a kid of any age to get them ready to start with a real fly rod is to give them a practice rod or "yarn rod." These outfits come with approximately twenty feet of heavy air-resistant line or rope to overweight the rod and slow things down. This enables you to feel the rod bend and make casts slowly. The thick line also helps you see it. These rods are approximately four feet long and don't need a reel. You can use them in a room with an eight-foot ceiling. If you don't have a yarn rod, you could take your rod apart and only use the top half.

Another one of Joan's teaching aids is horizontal, or ground casting. I often use it to teach kids but it works for beginning adult fly casters too. It's a drill to see and feel the casts for practice until we can do them overhead and learn the stroke overhead. Instead of looking up at the line against a bright sky, you can see the rod and line much more easily against green grass. The ease of visibility helps see what you're doing right or see and fix any mistakes.

The way I set up this drill is with four fluorescent orange mini sport cones to mark different points along imaginary lines and where to stand. I place three in a line fifty feet long; one in the middle and one at each end. The fourth cone, or caster place cone, should be placed a rod's length away from the middle cone to stand behind. In the accompanying photos, the author is doing the horizontal casting drill at one of two cones he placed sixty feet apart on a line of an athletic field. He will change directions and false cast to the other cone, and back and forth.

Now standing with both feet behind the caster, place cone and your rod held horizontally in front of you with twenty-five feet of line and leader extended. Point your rod 45 degrees to one side, then cast to the cone on the other side by moving the rod fast and stopping it about 45 degrees in that direction. Let the fly leader and line land and look at where they are and how straight the line and leader are laid out on the grass.

In this photo, the author is doing the horizontal casting drill at one of two cones he placed sixty feet apart on a line of an athletic field. He will change directions and false cast to the other cone, and back and forth. Photo: Edina Field.

They should land along the line leading to the cone fully extended and not in a pile. Now make a stroke in the other direction and stop the rod so the fly line lands toward that cone. After you can do this several times successfully, try casting without the fly touching the ground, with your fly line about three feet above the grass on both casts. Make a complete stop at the end of your stroke when your rod is pointing 45 degrees to the side and pause just long enough for the line and leader to almost fully straighten, then make your cast to the other side, and repeat. Try and make the loops identical when casting to either side.

When you can do this a half-dozen times back and forth without touching the ground with the fly or line, you've accomplished something. Here's a tip to help both casts keep the casts level. If you can find a utility wire, fence or roof line on a big building, try and follow the horizontal line with your rod tip.

This drill helps you discover that where and how firmly you stop the rod has an effect on the width of the loop produced. Cast with the rod tip moving over the imaginary straight line between the cones and vary the stroke so you can make wide ones or narrow loops at will. The motion of your casting arm is like when you're opening a door. If you "open the door" partially, the loop will be narrow, or if you open it all the way, the loop will be wide.

CHAPTER 4

ACCURACY

Chris Korich, has spent the last few years examining the best ways to teach and has mentored many winning ACA casters. Recently, Chris gave a teaching clinic at the Pittsburgh Casting Club and shared his fundamentals and in particular, his accuracy techniques. I also followed up later with specific questions to get some of his secrets. Compared to traditional orthodoxy, Chris's techniques are not in the mainstream but have proven very effective. Here are some of his main points for training and getting really good at accuracy casting.

Chris says the equipment is number one. It must be proportional to the size and strength of the caster. Pick-ups and lay-downs and false casting are fundamental. Your training should be a building process. Start casting to the first two targets at twenty-five and thirty-one feet and try and hit them three times in a row each before casting to the third at forty feet and so on. Train in thirty minute sessions, focusing on trying to build on consecutive hits on target. Practice should also be enjoyable. Take breaks in between sessions if you want to do an hour or so. Always try to end a session on a high note.

Chris teaches all students casting at targets to thread the line on their reel out the bottom instead of the top and make downward strips when lengthening line. This automatically teaches two things. First: How to make the hauling motion and coordinate a movement with the other hand while not interfering in the casting stroke. Second: How to do this and eliminate slack. After Maxine hit the far target in Bass Bug three times in a row in practice, someone asked, "How'd she do that?" And Chris exclaimed, "That's slack-free casting, baby!"

If you want to consistently hit the target, you need confidence and consistency in your

Chris Korich, a lefty, is casting with the foot of his casting arm forward. Righties would put their right foot forward to help align the body with the target.

form and routine. The way you stand when you cast helps you aim and prevents unwanted body motion. Unwanted motion is motion that is not away from, or directed at the target. If you are casting on land, a dock, or a boat deck and you want the best accuracy up to about fifty feet, use a staggered stance to establish a good base for balance.

I've taken notice of the body stance and movement of anglers and tournament casters and stance is an individual thing. Chris instructs students to point the foot on the casting side toward the target for good accuracy. He said it's just like a basketball player making a free throw. Keeping this foot forward helps align the body with the target. It can also act as a body block in distance casting since it helps prevent unwanted upper torso rotation. Most anglers keep the opposite foot forward since that is the preferred distance stance and easiest to perform any weight transfer. After learning your stroke and stance they will lock together, and if you're successful, you'll be able to point your toe at the target, close your eyes, and hit it! This makes a very good drill to incorporate into a practice routine.

Good casting accuracy gives you the ability to place a fly where you want it, with little deviation from the effects of wind. When I refer to "target" in accuracy, it may be a real target or the spot we visualize on the water where we want the fly to land. It might be inches or yards away from a fish, shoal of fish, or hiding place. If you can keep most casts within a thirty-inch diameter ring, up to fifty feet away, you have very good accuracy. I've invited instructors to cast at targets during ACA demos and even those very good casters have difficulties with the finite accuracy tasks. They would stop several feet above the target, as if casting to make a soft landing. Unfortunately, there is almost always some side wind to blow the fly off course.

Although tournament accuracy competitors need a strong lay-down, it is really helpful for most fishing applications too, especially in wind. Controlling the landing point of the fly requires three things. First, you must control the rod with adequate wrist and forearm strength to prevent sideways movements. The stroke, which correlates to the path of the hand, must compensate for wind drift too. If there is any rod tip deflection to either side, the loop will curve in or out, and the leader will not lay down straight. Second, the rod should be held close to vertical near your eyes, so you can best triangulate your aim and gravity will help turn over your leader and fly straight on target. Third, there must be enough line speed for complete leader straightening and minimal wind deviation. When it's windy, you're going to need to increase line speed with a faster stroke and by adding hauling.

Joan Wulff says if you're going to practice casting, you should use a target. It gives an aiming reference for the opposing back cast. If you enroll at her school, you'll cast at tournament hoops in her ponds. For accuracy practice, I recommend using targets. You can use 30-inch diameter hula hoops as targets or make them from ½-inch irrigation tubing and couplers. Wrap the black tubing with colored electrical tape for visibility.

Tim Rajeff says that tournament casting and its drills help you learn how to judge distance and adjust the length of your casting stroke to match the length of line you're casting. You'll need to do this with fixed lengths of line and then learn to aim while shooting and estimating distances.

If you first learn how to cast at targets, you'll be well equipped to use that skill in your fishing presentation. The casts in ACA are straight-line casts, no slack and no curves. There are many more advanced presentation casts that include slack and intentional curves which can help you deal with situations and catch fish. I'm not advocating a straight-line cast for all fishing presentations, but knowing how to make one will help when it comes to making slack line presentations.

These hoops are a set of regulation ACA thirty-inch hoops the author made for a few dollars and the two hundred-foot measuring tape to set up an accuracy course and measure distance casts.

Chris Korich taught me how to cast the ACA tournament fly accuracy games at the GGACC (Golden Gate Angling and Casting Club). He keeps his tournament tackle in a locker in the clubhouse and only takes it out two or three times a year to compete. He will usually shoot a few perfect scores in the accuracy events, which is extremely difficult to do.

One of the first things Chris taught me was the "free throw" stance, with the casting-side foot forward, in-line with the hip and shoulder. Next, he showed me his efficient "side-of-body" casting arm alignment with a near-vertical rod plane. As I detailed in the description of stroke mechanics, a near-vertical rod plane will help prevent a curved, or tucked layout of the line and leader, which will likely miss the target. Having the casting hand to the side of your head enables visual triangulation of the target and fly. This helps judge the distance of the cast in relation to the target.

Before you start casting, make sure your contact with the ground is solid and your body is balanced and relaxed. Notice the amount and direction of the wind. On the first casts at the target, lengthen the cast to adjust line length and hover the fly about five

Chris Korich is showing his arm and rod in the top-position.

feet over it. Most casters aim for the back of the rim. You might need to use "Kentucky Windage" on the long targets in a side-wind. That is, to compensate by aiming upwind as much as necessary to hit the target, depending on the amount of wind. Hovering is an old tournament accuracy technique used to see the fly better while measuring and aiming. You hover the fly by casting with enough forward line speed so the fly isn't already falling before it stops. You must let the leader turn over and the fly will almost hang, or hover momentarily.

This composite of casting in different casting planes shows the relation of the rod to the caster's eyes for aiming and the way the loop is affected by gravity.

Next, after approximating the right casting length, you should pin the line to the grip with the index finger and either lengthen or shorten the line until the length looks exact. To make final adjustments, lower the forward cast approximately one foot at a time until the fly is hovered about one foot above the center of the target. A good back cast is essential to eliminate drop or wind deviation. The back cast should be strong and have a tight loop. When you lower the front trajectory, you must raise the back, so they are 180 degrees opposed.

The last move is to "Cut the Cake." Center the rod, unrolling loop and fly, on a target on the lay-down. Visualizing it, you press down with a stiff wrist, like cutting a cake. The object is to get the leader to straighten completely, so the fly lands before the leader or line. This isn't a useless discipline. In fishing, this helps lengthen a dead drift, since it helps delay the line from bowing downstream.

To make a good lay-down, a fast, high back cast is required, to minimize the chance the unrolling leader will crash short of the target. You must aim so your leader unrolls inches above the target, or wind will blow your fly off the target. The lay-down in Dry Fly and Trout Fly Accuracy causes the fly to land harder than you'd typically want while dry-fly fishing for trout, but does aid in accurate placement in wind. In a fishing situation, you'd aim a foot higher and the energy will be dissipated so the fly will land softly.

Beginning casters often learn to consistently land their fly in line with the target, but can't get the distance right. Their leader crosses the centerline of the target but the fly is either a little long or short. Steve Rajeff taught me that all you have to do is know the distance between the targets and measure the line with hand strips before you cast. The targets are about six feet apart and you can use two small line strips or one huge one and shoot that amount into your cast at each successive target. Steve and most other seasoned tournament casters have learned to judge distance instinctively for most events.

It's fun and deadly to play with "measuring" if you know the right spacing. ACA has an old game called Wet Fly Accuracy that only allows a pick-up and lay-down and requires measured strips to extend the line between the targets. If your casting distance is off, use the cast as a reference and make the needed adjustment by releasing or stripping-in for the next cast. This is a useful skill when you're blind fishing a river. You work your fly across an imaginary grid a foot at a time until you've got it covered. That way, every fish in the pool or run has seen your fly.

When starting out, it's best to use smaller targets than the thirty-inch ACA targets. You can use any small object such as a Frisbee. The premise is that small adjustments are "steadier" than larger ones, therefore giving greater control over accuracy. Steve Rajeff said he imagines a mini-tornado spinning into the center of the target and with every false cast he makes it gets lower and lower and his fly gets progressively closer to the center of the target before he makes his lay-down. We all have a certain aiming point on our target during the hover. Steve says he aims for the back of the rim when casting at facilities designed with casting docks a foot or more above the water. Jay Clark, a good tournament caster, stated, "Hovering just over the front edge works on flat ground. Just remember, if you cast from an elevated position, the higher you are, the 'deeper' or further back in the target you'll need to aim."

When you can carry sufficient length in the air and false cast to your target, you'll be more accurate than when shooting line. When you have to shoot some line, you control distance by sight and feel. As you shoot line through the fingers of your line hand, you watch the loop and fly approach the target and have a couple of choices. You can let the cast "hit the reel," or come tight and turn over. If the amount of line you stripped off was exact, then good. If not, the cast will be short. Or, you can shoot line and regulate it with finger pressure to slow or stop it where you want the fly to land.

CHANGE-OF-DIRECTION CAST

When you finish a swing or a drift in flowing water and want to reposition the fly upstream, it is best to make an easy, efficient Change-of-Direction cast. Change-of-Direction casts are also required if you're trying to methodically fan-cast and cover stillwaters or saltwater. There are many choices of casts and some are more suitable for certain situations than others.

The most basic and tedious change of direction cast is the Star Cast. It is false casting incrementally in a circle until you've reached your desired change of direction. If you're not in hurry and want to dry a fly in the process, you might use this one.

You can use water tension instead of making a back cast to make a change of direction cast. If your fly is awash downstream and you want to make a short upstream cast, you can slowly accelerate the rod and cast against the resistance of the current on the line, leader, and fly. As the fly breaks the surface, make the forward stroke. This is called a Tension Cast. This is the simplest way to make short casts with tandem rigs and heavy nymphs.

The Belgian cast can be used as a Change-of-Direction cast. It is performed by picking up the fly and swinging the rod-tip sidearm in an oval path into the back cast and up to a near vertical position with constant tension that ends with a stop in the direction of the intended target. The back cast never stops, so it does not straighten out. You do not have to present the fly on the forward cast and can change to making straight false casts.

The Wye cast, named after a UK river, uses a Belgian cast to change directions. To make the Wye cast, pick up the fly from downstream and turn your body in the direction of your target while making an oval back cast 180 degrees opposite your target. Let the back cast straighten, then make your delivery.

CHAPTER 5

DISTANCE CASTING

In most fly-fishing situations, a majority of the fish are caught at close range under thirty feet. If you can carefully approach feeding trout and get that close it will help make your cast more accurate than trying at sixty feet. Striped bass often feed in the trough of a sandy beach in the surf, right at your feet. On the other hand, on a calm day, fish like permit or bonefish are shy of moving shadows and sounds like a push-pole on crunching coral or waves on a boat hull. They'll spook before you can get within casting range.

Presenting the fly further away from the sound and sight of your boat often means the difference between a hooked and a departed fish. Being a little further away also prevents fish from spooking at the sight of you waving your rod. Sight fishing often means that if you can see the fish, the fish can see you too.

When fishing in a river, a long cast provides a longer swing in the current, or a longer retrieve before the fly reaches your rod tip. Not only can you cover more water with a longer cast, but it can result in more bites from species that often follow before striking. If you're wading, anchored, or staked-up and don't have time to wade or move the boat closer to a fish, the ability to cast farther gives more opportunities.

WIND AND TRAJECTORY

Whenever you're trying to get the most distance from your cast, you should try to get the wind in your favor and cast at the optimal trajectory, or angle. When trying to throw a football or baseball as far as possible, you face these same challenges. Ideally, you want to aim the trajectory so the loop and leader unroll, then lose momentum just before landing. Paul Arden, the British instructor and rod manufacturer, says he aims his casts at real or imaginary "sky" targets for back casts and long delivery casts.

Delivering your fly downwind is usually advantageous for distance. The stronger the wind at your back, the higher you can aim your delivery cast, to a point. If you aim so high that the leader straightens and falls many feet straight down before landing, you've aimed too high and probably lost a few feet of casting distance. If you aim too low, you will shorten distance potential. When there is little wind, it's better to cast level. We see what happens to casts made on different trajectories when we're pegging the landing point of the flies and measuring the casts at the National Championships.

We even have to factor gravity vs. favorable air and wind conditions in the trajectory of our casts. All other variables being equal, casting trajectory should also vary with line density and fly weight and resistance. High-density sinking lines are less air resistant than floating lines and will need a higher trajectory to make a longer flight than a more air-resistant line of the same weight. Casting with a big, air-resistant fly requires a lower trajectory. Some things you can't change, like the weather; other things like casting angle and trajectory, you can.

The assistance of wind behind a cast can add many feet to our distance. Wind against our casts can cause them to stall completely. Use wind to your advantage for safety, distance, and less effort. Try to wade or position a boat to present your fly downwind for best advantage. It will be harder to back cast into the wind but a last false cast isn't as far as a forward cast shot into the distance. The next best option is a quartering angle with the wind on the side of your line hand. It will keep the fly away from you and still help sail your line and fly in your casting direction.

Casting downwind reduces air resistance in frontal areas because of decreased relative speed, and the wind pulls and pushes the cast downwind. The backside of a loop has a concave surface like a sail. The two most desired ACA Nationals host clubs when a caster wants to set a distance record are Long Beach, California near the Pacific coast, and Toronto, Canada, sitting above Lake Ontario. These bodies of water are weather-making wind generators and can produce humidity, which is also helpful for distance casting. High altitude also increases casting distance because it makes the air thinner, decreasing air resistance. This effect has been proven at the International Sportmen's Expositions and Best of the West 5-weight competitions in the Rocky Mountains, compared to the casts at the California ISE competition near sea level. The casting distance of the same competitors was greater at high altitude.

The way I like beginning casters to advance to distance casting is to first learn to carry adequate line in the air without hauling. Or if it's a shooting head, learn to false cast and regulate overhang. This isolates any shortcomings first or confirms they are ready to move forward. Then I like to teach them double-hauling which is a quite exhilarating at first. After they demonstrate good double-hauling, I teach them to match stroke and haul length with casting distance. Finally, I teach them the most advantageous use of body movement and a few other tips.

Carrying line means to false cast the head plus a significant amount of running line. You can carry line with or without hauling but double-hauling makes it possible to carry longer lengths of line in the air than without it. This is essential for distance casts with an integrated head weight-forward line with a running line. You will have a limit to how much line you can shoot into your delivery, so you can usually add the additional amount you can carry to the total distance you can cast. When you use shooting heads with mono or super thin shooting line, you can't carry as much because the thin line makes the loop unstable. The amount of line I like beginners to carry is usually a short or medium weight-forward head plus about fifteen feet of running line. Let's say, sixty feet plus the leader. This will show proficiency or show any flaws. In time, with practice, you might work that up to eighty feet or more!

To start learning distance, try extending false casts until the head of a weight-forward line is beyond the rod tip without hauling. Use a floating weight forward line with a head of around forty. Don't use a long head or steelhead taper. Their heads are about sixty-seven feet long. Pinch the line to the cork with the index finger of your casting hand. Look at the loop size and try to make them about three feet wide. If you can't make them at least three feet wide, practice on a few more occasions until you can before moving on to learn hauling. If you want to be objective about your distance and increasing it, buy a two hundred-foot measuring tape reel to measure distance casts. You can also use it to set your accuracy target distances.

DISTANCE STROKE

In a test between strength versus form in distance casting, form wins. In fly distance casting, back cast and forward cast alignment must be perfect or the forward cast loop will fall over or sideways and ruin the cast. The most efficient casting stroke leaves the least margin for misalignment, but it also takes the most explosive strength. Great casters extend the effective stroke length with weight transfer and body movement. Generally, beginning or weaker casters require a longer stroke to reach their longest casts. Accuracy is different.

I learned from casting shooting heads that form is essential for distance casting and brute strength isn't the answer. You'll realize that all-out effort ruins form. My friend, ACA and international distance champion Henry Mittel, describes the degrees of effort in a cast as under-powered, normal, maximum, and excessive. After exceeding the maximum amount of effort to put into a cast, you will see how excess will hurt your tracking and cost you distance. Using good form with concentration and smoothness will get you farther than just hitting it hard like a game of strength. The role strength plays in casting has been misunderstood and I hope to clarify it.

Since there is a wide variation in the size, strength, speed, and flexibility of those who learn fly casting, there will be differences in physical ability. You should choose a style of distance casting stroke that is a good match for you individually. If you are fast, long limbed, and strong, and use stiff rods, a compact stroke will probably give the best results. If on the other hand, you do not have these characteristics, or favor softer rod actions, a much longer distance stroke will help realize better results.

Long stroke length decreases severity of angle between the rod tip and the fly line. This makes it easier to accelerate the line and is why someone with less strength usually uses a longer stroke than a stronger caster. A person with less strength may be able to reach high line speeds with a longer stroke and a rod with a softer action and achieve comparable distances.

When you're casting at targets up to about fifty feet away, you mainly use rotation in your stroke to make the cast. For distance, however, I'd like to interject the idea of stroke length. If for example your rod hand moves forward and back eighteen inches during a fifty-foot false cast, I'd like it to move thirty inches forward from the back stop to the forward stop for a seventy-five-foot cast. This would be increasing the stroke length.

The radius of the imaginary circle your hand moves around will also have to be larger as you cast farther and increase stroke length, or in other words, the path of your rod hand needs to be straighter. Here's an axiom from instructor Bill Gammel: The shorter the cast, the shorter the stroke; the longer the cast, the longer the stroke. If you don't do this when imparting high-rod speed, the rod will not be able to handle the sudden bending and will send waves into the loop that ruin the cast. (This is also covered in Chapter 7: Troubleshooting.)

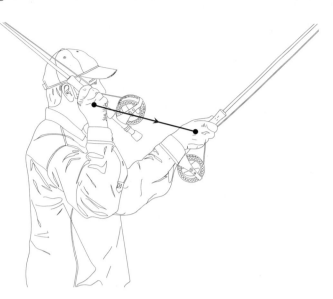

The short stroke is suitable for a short cast.

When a caster makes a false cast or makes short- to medium-length casts, she uses her muscles to contract and stop the rod to make a tight loop. When she makes a long delivery cast, she doesn't limit the forward stroke with a stop in that manner. The caster stops the rod at the end of cast when she "runs out of arm" as she rotates the wrist, then snaps the elbow straight. Stopping the rod at the right point makes a tight loop. Stopping lower,

The long stroke will help you make a long cast.

or later, increases the size of the loop. What the caster does after the loop is formed also has an influence on keeping the loop tight and aerodynamic. Stop the rod, then lift the rod tip a little to tighten the loop.

In the quest to achieve good distance, begin to learn and practice with a careful, smooth stroke. When you've gotten the mechanics down and start casting with more acceleration, you will experiment using your maximum effort and find the point of negative returns. Just back off a little until you find your best speed and control.

For the sake of simplicity, the length of a casting stroke should be only as long as required to cast the length of line used. The stroke length is also related to the rod action. When false-casting before a distance presentation, the false-cast stroke and any hauling should start proportional to the length of the actual cast and therefore not your longest final delivery cast, which will have your longest effort, stroke, haul, and body movement as you shoot line.

To make that delivery cast, there should be changes to body and arm position to keep the rod moving straight through one casting plane in order to maximize line acceleration in the proper direction. The object is to accelerate, then stop the rod to

The slight repositioning of the rod after the stop helps increase the length of stroke of the delivery cast.

produce a tight, fast loop. This is produced and controlled mainly by the stroke, or path of the casting hand.

In distance casting, both the back cast and the forward cast stroke must be lengthened. There are two ways to start the stroke further rearward to increase the stroke arc, by bringing the rod hand further back on the last back cast before the stop, or by drifting. Drifting is a rearward repositioning of the rod hand during the pause after the back cast stop to lengthen the stroke of the following forward delivery cast. This movement should be about three inches or less, otherwise you will be adding slack. Instead of a rearward move and an increase in stroke length, you can rotate the wrist backward and slightly open the rod arc. Next, I'll describe a distance cast delivery sequence in detail.

The forward delivery on a long-distance cast should start with slightly increased grip pressure during smooth acceleration of the rod with a long simultaneous haul. The muscles of the body will be contracted and effort should be made to stabilize the rod in hand to track straight ahead. As rod bending is sensed by the wrist, it should open to add the final rotation.

Stopping the rod and controlling the loop should begin by contracting your arm muscles so you straighten your arm, increase grip pressure, and straighten your wrist. This should produce rod rotation and high line speed. At the same time, the hauling hand should release the line near mid-thigh and it will shoot line into the cast. As the speed of the line overtakes the straightening rod tip, the loop is formed. As the wrist of your rod hand passes a straight position, as does the rod, you should thrust the rod forward and slightly upward. This movement is called Thrusting and helps tighten the loop. After the Thrust, relax your rod hand.

To increase your delivery speed for more distance, you must use your body properly and make the appropriate length stroke and haul for your potential. Depending upon your strength and speed as described in the previous sections, you will either be more productive using a long, or a short casting stroke. Whichever you use, you must accelerate the cast smoothly. In the Western tournament style of casting, you will want to lead with the elbow

Finishing a distance cast by fully extending and raising the casting arm and bending the wrist down slightly is called a Thrust. It helps tighten the loop and extend casting distance. Photo: Edina Field.

and have approximately two 90-degree joint angles before making a long cast. The first is at the shoulder; the second is at the elbow. This is the same relationship as the arm positions before making a baseball pitch.

For casting integrated floating lines with rods designed for fishing, not the stiff "pool cues" the ACA and ICSF casters use for distance events with shooting heads, most casters use a much longer stroke to maximize distance. The stroke many use is called the 170-degree stroke and uses a rod arc of 170 degrees. The object is to delay wrist rotation until near the end of the stroke and thrust the rod to a stop in each direction with full arm extension. With this cast, competitive casters can carry more than ninety feet of line!

The greater the length of the compound movements in the stroke, the more chances for tracking errors. So, if you have a long stroke, you will need to compensate to maintain one casting plane from front to back. For longer casts, open the casting shoulder joint to increase the range of motion and the upper arm will be approximately 90 degrees to the cast on the back cast, before forward delivery.

Since the longest stroke is the full extension of the arm and body on the forward delivery, the caster should check it for proper tracking. Many of us have a tendency to rotate at the waist for extension and cross our casting arm over before the end of the stroke, instead of forward toward the target. It shouldn't look like the follow-through of a baseball pitcher. The best way to keep the delivery movement straight is to turn at the waist, open the shoulder, and reach in the direction of the target.

RELEASE AND SHOOTING LINE

The optimum time to release the fly line is the moment you've stopped the rod. The size of the resulting loop and thus the distance of the cast will suffer if your release is too early or too late. If it's too early, you'll lose power and get some slack in the line. It you release too late, the loop will open up.

When you release the line and shoot it into a cast, you can leave the line alone and let it run up the guides, or you can release it through an opening between the tips of your index and thumb in the shape of an "O," or let it run through your hand on your other finger tips under your thumb. You can pitch it and stop it when you wish. Stopping it is how to limit the length of the cast and drop the fly where you want it. Using the "O" when your object is distance can prevent a tangle but using it as a guide creates some resistance and lessens distance.

MAXIMUM DOUBLE-HAUL

Nothing can add more line speed to a good cast than good hauling. A tight loop cast with high line speed will achieve maximum distance. The most important factors for good hauling are timing, length, and speed. For a maximum-length cast, move the line hand toward the stripping guide to pinch the line before the haul. When I begin my forward cast, my line hand is over my head. Make the downward haul smoothly to coincide with the fast rod stroke and the travel of the line hand should continue down to the thigh on the same side before you release the line. After the release, the hand should follow through unless the fingers of the line hand are used as a line guide.

USING THE BODY

Body movement can increase casting distance in four ways. It can increase line tension in the cast, help get the casting arm and rod moving in the direction of the cast, and increase the effective length of the stroke. If the waist is used to bend back and forth in addition to leg movement, it can also add to the total casting arc and stroke length.

If you can use body movement to assist casting without spooking your quarry, it will help you make longer casts. There are times when lower body movement will scare fish and other situations when it won't. For example, you wouldn't want to send out waves when wading in a calm trout pool. If instead you're on a large enough boat like a flats skiff or center console, or on land, you can use body movement with little regard for scaring the fish. When wading in current, you don't have much choice in your stance. You pretty much have to stand sideways to the flow to deflect water and reduce drag. You might be limited to only using the movement of your upper body and trunk to assist.

Your stance is the foundation for a long cast. Extending your base increases stability and allows you to effectively transfer your body weight in the direction of your casts. A movement of the body toward the direction of the cast helps accelerate the arms and the rod in making a cast. Weight transfer is essential in using heavy tackle, overcoming wind, and increasing casting distance. Different stances set the limits for the range of body movement and help prevent excessive movement.

The standard distance stance is to put the line hand side foot forward, which creates a body block to push against and enables the most travel. To increase the length of movement away from and toward the casting direction, rotate your shoulder and hips in conjunction with transferring your weight. Be careful and maintain good tracking of your stroke in line with the cast; a lot of body rotation can throw it off.

The distance casting sequence including body movement should start by opening your stance so your foot is forward on your line-hand side and the back foot is pointing outward. Start with a slight bend in the knees and weight back. Start false casting and hauling while transferring your body weight fore and aft with the rotational torso movements. If you have good flexibility, bend slightly backward at the waist during the back cast and

Using weight transfer by moving your weight to the rear during the back cast and forward to make the forward cast. Photo: Edina Field.

forward on the forward casts. At this point, you will be either shooting line into both the forward cast and back cast—if you have an integrated head line—or adjusting the overhang if casting a shooting head.

When all elements including wind, line length, aim, and trajectory are right, start to make the delivery at the end of your back cast when you feel or see the timing cues to start moving everything in the casting direction. This will be that the back cast is almost perfectly straight but not noticeably falling. The body should move just before the forward stroke. Start the delivery by bending the knees more deeply, arch the torso even more and transfer your weight to the back foot.

Start the stroke and push forward with the long edge of the back foot while driving the body rotation and extension forward and upward in the direction of the cast. As you make the stroke, use your weight transfer and the forward extension of your legs, trunk, shoulders, and arm. This movement in the direction of the cast increases rod rotation and can have a significant effect on line speed.

SHOOTING HEADS

My initial interest in tournament distance casting with shooting heads was aimed at helping me cast farther for stripers in the North East. I had little interest in competing. As a matter of fact, the first tournament I went to was in San Francisco in 2003, and I brought a video camera on a tripod and my 10-weight fishing rod. I was only going to take video until Chris Korich made me enter Angler's Fly Distance with that rod.

After breaking the ice, I flew out many times and trained with all the ACA distance record holders on the West Coast. We never had a talent hotbed of distance casters at that level in the East. After I learned these shooting-head distance techniques, I fished with top striper guides and became known for catching big stripers from boats with long casts and big flies.

Integrated fly lines have more inherent stability and self-correct flight defects caused by minor tracking deviation. Shooting heads are not as forgiving, especially if they lack a rear taper, or both the front and rear tapers, as is the case in some level heads. They have a tendency to pile if the acceleration isn't smooth and the tracking isn't true.

The speed of the line, the amount of overhang, and line design determine the rate of loop turnover. Overhang is the length of running or shooting line extended from the tip-ring to the head while casting. When a tight loop is unrolling, the end is moving forward and its shape cuts through the air. The longer the unrolling is delayed and forward momentum continues, the farther the cast will go.

Increased head length increases the potential length of a cast in two ways. It delays loop opening and if you carry the additional length before release, it adds directly to the cast length. Let's say you can false cast a thirty-foot head and shoot sixty feet of running line regardless of head length and it will turn over completely. You'll cast ninety feet, plus leader. Now if you can cast a forty-foot head that weighs the same, it will directly add ten feet to the cast. You can now cast one hundred feet, plus the leader. A longer front-taper delays opening too, but if it's too long, it might not open at all. If a line is designed without any front taper, the line will kick hard and the turnover will be fast and abrupt. So, for increased distance, select lines or heads with the longest belly you can carry in the air and reasonable front taper that will turn over.

Overhang affects the cast in two ways. First, the length of overhang adds to the total length of line you are carrying and to total casting distance. Secondly, adding overhang delays turnover. There is a point of negative returns when increasing the overhang. If the overhang is too long, the line will get wavy and unstable and the loop will collapse on the delivery. Use a short overhang in low-wind conditions, starting with about three feet so the head doesn't enter the tip guide when false-casting. The loop should look normal and smooth. Increase overhang length in higher wind until you find the sweet spot without the wiggles. That should be around ten feet or so in length.

DISTANCE TRAINING

To improve, and not lose what you've learned, you should practice year-round, even on snow if your region receives any. Don't expect miracles, or even progress, without putting in time and concentration. If you have good form, your muscles will get conditioned and you'll be able to handle stiffer rods, heavier lines, and cast farther with time. Regularly measure your distance casts after making any changes to your cast to compare the difference.

If you want to perform some exercises to increase your stroke and hauling speed, here's one Chris Korich taught me at the 2004 Northwestern Tournament in San Francisco. You can do this drill even if you don't have room for a back cast. Ideally you want to work up to about forty feet of fly line extended, plus the leader. If you can't cast that far, work up to it. Make sure your casting forearm is vertical, or even angled slightly back. (Refer to Chapter 3: Cast Basics for more detail on roll-cast form.) This arm position will include and condition your deltoid muscles and as you pull down, even your *latissimus dorsi*. Do this for forty minutes every session as often as your schedule can accommodate. Chris reassured me of the resistance this drill offers. "Remember, your rod and reel might not weigh five pounds plus, but your arm surely does." You can do this drill on water or lawn.

Another way to train for increased distance is progressive distance training on the grass. Pick a spot where you can control your position in relation to the wind. First, cast with the wind on your line hand side and 90 degrees to your casting direction. This way, the drill will

Chris likes to use the roll cast to condition the muscles as light training for distance casting. Here he is roll-casting at targets.

not favor either your back cast or your forward cast and you can train equally. Second, you can cast downwind, which will help you measure tracking accurately with no side wind and its affects. The wind at your back will help you develop a strong back cast and will also let you realize good loop turnover on the forward cast.

Start by warming up and then cast as far as possible without compromising your form. Measure the cast and note the wind speed. End the session and repeat another day. Each session, try to incrementally increase your distance until you run out of line. If you're casting downwind, take variances in wind speed into account. You can cast around 30 percent farther in a good wind than in calm. Set realistic goals based on your physical condition and the amount of time you can practice. Also practice casting directly into a brisk wind to help increase your ability. Remember to make your forward cast low into the wind and your back cast high casting with the wind.

Good form is more important in distance casting than muscle, but once you've gotten the form and timing perfected, the only way to increase your casting distance is by physical conditioning. We are typically at our physical prime in our twenties, but it takes time to develop skill. I've seen remarkable casting by anglers and competitors over fifty. On average, fifty years of age is when adults start losing muscle mass without exercising to maintain it. The legs are the first to go! ACA has Senior Men's and Senior Women's Divisions and many of the distance records are close to the Men's Division. We've had competitors in their nineties! These participants maintain good technique. Near the end of this book I'll provide some specific advice on how to resistance train to make fast, controlled, stroke and hauling motions. Consult with your physician before doing any strenuous drills or exercises described in this book.

The main muscles used in casting are in the forearm, triceps, deltoids, and *latissimus dorsi*. The legs muscles help with rapid weight transfer. The stomach muscles are also important if you have a healthy back and can use spinal flexibility to assist your casts. The way to work the upper body is to perform high-resistance, low-repetition exercises with professional guidance. This should stimulate fast-twitch muscle fiber, which helps achieve good hand speed. When you can't reach the gym, use hand and forearm exercisers like the Powerball, Digi-flex, or various coil-spring grips. Don't forget to rest a day between strenuous sessions. There is a list of exercises later on.

CHAPTER 6

FISHING CASTS

To become a good tournament caster, you should master the basics of line handling, accuracy, distance, dealing with wind, and more. To become a good angler, you should combine these skills with casts and techniques that help you present a variety of flies with a variety of tackle in a way that will fool and catch fish. Tim Rajeff says the object of practice is getting to the point where you only think of where you want the fly to land. If you only fish for one species in one body of still or moving water, your job is easier. If you travel or pursue different species of fish, maybe in a variety of waters, you'll have to research and learn new things.

In tournament casting we mostly use floating lines for accuracy and sinking lines for distance events. When you're fishing and expecting to make long casts you have to take care not to tangle running or shooting line that is stripped out ready to shoot, or you'll miss opportunities. As I mentioned before, the larger the coils, the less likely a tangle is to result. Also, the line should be arranged so the line is shot through the stripper guide from the top of the stack of coils to the bottom. Also take precautions to remove objects in a boat, on the ground, or on your person that might catch the line and interrupt the cast.

Regardless of whether you're fishing from a boat, float tube, dock, while wading, or from land, there are three ways to keep the line ready. First, stripping large loops onto a boat deck, the ground, or the dock. Second, using a stripping basket, and lastly, by holding loops in your line hand.

If you're going to fish from the bow of a flats skiff, putting the line in the cockpit (which is lower than the casting platform) places it out of the wind and away from your casting area. It also prevents the line from blowing off the deck and into the water. If you have to fish from the stern of a boat that has tangling hazards, a free-standing stripping basket can be a help. A stripping basket worn around the waist is commonly used when surf or lake casting while wading or climbing a rock jetty. A stripping basket usually has line fingers on the inside pointing up to help keep the coils open and to prevent line from sliding and tangling. If you wade deep enough, however, the basket will annoy you by floating up on your waist. My favorite ones are sold by Orvis and HMH. My second favorite is the first one I made before commercial ones and it is made from a Rubbermaid dish basin, a bungee cord, and line trimmer fingers.

If on the other hand, you wade in rivers or streams and make long casts, holding coils of line in thc line hand will be optimal, since a basket would drag and fill with water in current.

This is an Orvis stripping basket, which is useful to prevent tangles and to keep current from pulling your running or shooting line away while wading. Photo: Edina Field.

Some saltwater waders prefer holding the line instead of using a basket. The way to arrange the coils is to strip in and coil around six feet of line and hold it between the last two fingers of the line hand. This one should touch the water so tension prevents it from fouling on the way up the guides. Some call this the River Loop. The next loop, slightly smaller, goes between the next set of fingers until you are holding up to, say, four coils in descending size. When you shoot the line, release each loop by reducing the pressure in each set of fingers until the cast is away. Hopefully it doesn't foul. After I've addressed casting in a variety of situations, I'm going to address casting a variety of lines and flies.

Casting virtually weightless practice yarn flies or light dry flies is a pleasure. The leader turns over gracefully and the fly lands softly. However, when you fish you may have to use sinking lines, weighted flies, tandem flies, wind-resistant flies, split shot, or steel-bite tippet. Weight on the leader causes

Instead of using a line or stripping baskets, the author is holding coils. Many anglers prefer holding coils of line when fishing in rivers. Photo: Edina Field.

hinging, kicking, and various dangerous collisions and accidental hookings. Slinging weight causes more speed and energy in the turnover. Wind-resistant flies, on the other hand, slow down line speed and the turnover of the cast. You have to mitigate the effects differently according to what you're casting.

In the case of casting with weight on the line, slow down the line speed in the cast by casting a wider loop. This will help make the cast smoother and prevent the leader from acting like a sling shot. You will need to adjust your pause timing since the weight might cause rapid turnover. Therefore, you might have to begin the next cast a little earlier.

Another good cast for preventing tangles or getting hit by heavy rigs is the Belgian cast described in change of direction casts. It uses an oval back cast without a stop in the back cast and keeps tension on the line until the stop for the delivery cast.

The last method to prevent personal collision is to tilt the rod tip away and cast side arm, so the line's path is away from you. Do adjust your trajectory and try and prevent the back cast from hitting any surface that might cause damage or ruin the forward cast. Also, gravity will act faster on the additional weight and the fly will fall faster.

In the case of wind-resistant flies, you will need to increase line speed to overcome the wind drag. Heavy-dressed saltwater or muskie flies have both drag and weight. In addition, they hold water weight when you lift them out of the water to cast. Poppers for bass are usually pretty light but have significant air and water resistance too. You have to slowly strip them off the water or they will make a big burping sound, which can scare fish. One trick to get a popper in the air softly is to do a forward roll cast and once it's airborne, make a back cast. To cope with casting wind-resistant flies, use more pace in your stroke and maximize the length and speed of your double-haul. If you can do it without scaring the fish, put your body into it as in a distance cast.

In the previous chapter I covered distance casting with high-density sinking shooting heads and monofilament shooting lines. These heads are connected with knots and provide for quick changes. Lines with integrated heads and running lines don't have these knots and run through your fingers and guides without a problem. Some integrated lines now have loop-to-loop connection for interchangeable tips, but that is close to the front of the line.

When you use shooting heads for fishing, you'll have to take precautions not to get line connections caught or damaged by the guides. The way to do this is to point the rod tip at your fly when you are stripping or retrieving line, or in the direction of a running fish.

A line that sinks makes lifting it to the surface for a pick-up more difficult than a floating line. You can either strip in enough line to pick it up, or make one or more roll casts to get it to the surface, then pick it up out of the water. When swinging a sinking line in a strong current, the resistance automatically brings it up if you let it hang downstream.

DEPTH AND SPEED CONTROL IN MOVING WATER

Most of what I've written to this point applies to straight casts and retrieves without moving water. When you cast across a river or stream, the current bellies the line and carries it below the fly, often speeding the fly along faster and faster. The angle that you cast in relation to current has an effect on the drift speed in the case of a floating presentation, or the depth and speed in the case of a presentation below the surface.

The greater the angle you cast upstream when fishing a floating presentation, the more this drag will eventually occur if you do not counteract it. The initial drift is slower because the current will cause slack but it will later cause a belly in the line, which will pull on the leader. Drag is when the line pulls the fly faster across the surface than the speed of the water it is floating on. Not only does casting across stream create slack between the rod tip and fly, but it may create a faster-than-desirable drift speed. There are some cases when you want to drift a fly downstream at the same speed as the current it sits in without imparting movement. This is called a dead drift. If the leader is not interfering with the drift, it is called drag-free. Most presentations for trout which imitate mayflies on the surface require a drag-free drift.

In other cases, you may want to give movement to the fly and tow it across the surface like a water skier. The greater the angle downstream you cast, the faster the fly will drift under tension and the shorter the duration of a drag-free drift. If you want to increase drift speed, make your casts at least forty-five degrees downstream. There are ways to slow the line and fly to get a dead drift, or drag-free drift.

To make that dead drift, make a steep cast with a high back cast so the fly lands before the line or drag will start prematurely. Make your cast approximately 45 degrees downstream and immediately after you stop the rod and before the line lands, swing the rod upstream so the

The author, who is right handed, has made a reach mend upstream after the stop. The reach mend helps prevent fly drag on moving water. Photo: Edina Field.

This is a side-by-side comparison of performing a reach mend to the right of the angler and to the left of the angler as seen from the front. Photo: Chris Theising.

rod tip is pointing 45 to 90 degrees upstream. Then lower the rod tip so it almost touches the water. This is called a reach mend. You will need to perform this cast to your left and to your right, depending upon which side of the river you're on. Follow the fly downstream by pointing your rod tip at it unless you detect drag.

If you see drag and a downstream bow in the line, lift the back half of the line, trying not to disturb the fly, and flip it upstream so you straighten out the bow in the line. It can be performed to the left or right of the caster, depending upon which side of the river she's on. This is called a water mend. You may do this more than once if you're careful. Continue following the fly with your rod tip as it floats downstream until it is unfishable. Hopefully all this will be abbreviated by the rise of a fish taking your fly.

This maneuver is an upstream flip of the line after it has landed on the water. This mend also helps prevent the fly from dragging and can be performed more than once during a drift. Photo: Edina Field.

Casting angle in relation to the current requires more considerations when using a sinking fly compared to a floating line and fly. In the case of sinking lines and flies, the farther upstream you cast them, the deeper they will initially sink. This changes as the line gets downstream of you and the water resistance pulls them upwards in the water column. They will end up close to or on the surface if you wait. Be ready, since fish often grab a fly as it ascends.

When you're making a downstream dead drift or an active swing, follow the fly downstream with your rod tip to eliminate slack. You will be able to feel any contact better that way and be able to keep a fish on the hook. If you're fishing deep by starting with an upstream cast to let the fly sink and you want to add speed to your fly, lead the fly with the rod tip below it downstream, gently pulling faster than the current. This works best with a short line.

THE SALTWATER QUICK CAST

The ACA has an accuracy fly event called Bass Bug Accuracy. It teaches us to double-haul and shoot line with a minimum of false casts to targets. Casting from the fifth target at fifty feet to the sixth one at seventy feet requires good skill, especially in wind. This helps prepare us for certain fishing situations when we must be able to quickly make long, accurate casts before fish leave or spook from you or your boat.

Whether you're sight fishing on shore, wading, or from the deck of a flats skiff, you must have the advantage of surprise. When permit, tarpon, and bonefish are spooked, they will leave

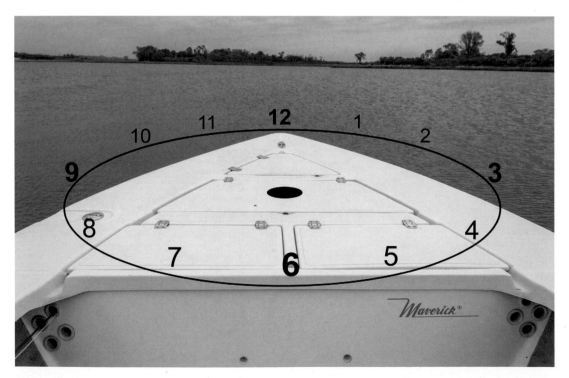

The clock orientation on the front deck of a flats skiff used between angler and guide to communicate the location of fish and other features. Photo: Chris Theising.

in a hurry and possibly spook every other form of life on a flat too. Besides these tropical flats species, you can sight fish in shallow water for striped bass, sharks, redfish, carp, trout, and other species as well.

An experienced and considerate skipper operating a flats skiff will often try to push the boat into an angle for good visibility to eliminate glare and to let you make a good cast with a favorable wind to a fish. But in many instances, that is impossible. Sometimes the tide on a flat makes it necessary to cast against the wind or look toward the sun. It's also the job of the captain to call out the location of the fish he wants you to see using the numbers on a clock face and other relative objects. He might say, "see that that big white spot at 2 o'clock? Two bones are about to cross it!"

The reference for the center of this clock is the center of casting deck or platform on the bow. Ideally casts should be made at 10 o'clock or 11 o'clock for a right-hander. This provides the safest cast for your boat mates, the lowest chance of detection by the fish, an opportunity to adjust the boat angle, and the possibility of multiple shots. Fish that intercept the boat will spook from it. Fish approaching from your dominant, or casting side, will often require a back-hand cast. If the fish is at 12 o'clock, present with a sidearm cast that won't hit the guide on the poling platform at 6 o'clock! Or, if there is time and it won't spook the fish, the guide can push the boat into a safe casting angle with the bow facing 2 o'clock for a right-handed caster.

The Saltwater Quick Cast routine helps the angler organize equipment in a state of readiness to minimize the time to safely and accurately present the fly. The object is to present the fly with the minimum number of false casts in order to accelerate, extend, and shoot the line. The first thing in the order of actually performing this cast is to consider the running line. It has to be ready to flow smoothly through your hands and guides. If it won't, it will blow the shot.

Your fly line must be absolutely clean and in good condition. Additionally, all line connections must be strong but streamlined, so they will pass through the guides without catching. I recommend washing fly lines in warm soapy water every three days of use in the saltwater. I also carry a terry face cloth and some fresh water onboard to run a line through if I feel dried salt on it. Even if a manufacturer states their line has built-in lubricant, I'll clean and apply Glide line-cleaner and lubricant at night before retiring to count jumping tarpon. I'll let it dry overnight and in the morning, I'll buff the line with a dry terry and reel it up, ready to go.

One I've stripped out the length of line I need onto the deck of a boat or into my basket, I stretch all of it between my hands and make a clearing cast. That's when you cast it out and strip it in. In a skiff, I carefully make the largest coils I can in the left side of the cockpit behind the casting platform. I stop arranging the coils of line with about two rod lengths of line, plus the leader, extended past the rod tip. I hold the fly hook by the bend between the index and thumb of my line hand with the point facing away. This is for safety. Control the line leading up to your stripping-guide with the index finger of the rod hand. You can now shake another rod length of line out of the rod tip, so the large loop of line just grazes the water. You will have about twenty feet of fly line ready to begin the Saltwater Quick Cast. The following description is for your longest cast. You won't need as many false casts or hauls for a close cast.

The direction of the first cast depends upon the wind direction. Wind blowing in the direction of the cast helps straighten the line and provide resistance for the next cast before much line is out. Wind blowing against the first cast would prevent the line from going out and waste time.

If the wind is in your face, start with a back cast and hold the hook away at an angle so the wind won't swing it into you. If the wind is behind you, start with a forward overhead cast or a roll cast. Let the

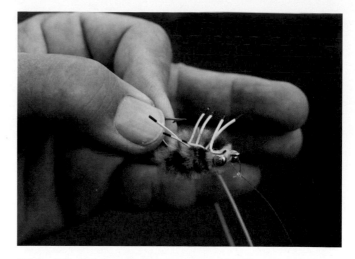

Holding a fly and the end of his line while sight fishing enables you to safely release the fly, and doubling the leader helps you get the fly to the fish faster. Photo: Edina Field.

cast pull the hook out and away from the fingers of your line hand and let the wind straighten the line and leader. If you wish, you can even let the fly anchor briefly for resistance against the rod to "water load" the cast. Double-haul and shoot as much line as possible on two to three false casts and release and shoot the presentation cast using an O-ring with your hand to keep better control of the line. Make sure to maintain high line speed and no slack. It your fly hits the water, try shooting less line, raise the trajectory or shorten your pause. You can even use your back cast for the delivery. The back cast is also the best way to cast to a fish on your rod side, especially if it's a close shot.

Tim Rajeff also has some suggestions on things to practice and learn for the flats. He likes to teach how to deliver casts to fish with the minimum of false casts too, but will even use a stop watch in practice to help reduce delivery time. You have to be able to make deliveries at various distances and Tim reminds students to learn to change stroke length while changing cast distance.

He says change-of-direction and change-of-distance casts are very important to practice separately and together. He recommends making a medium cast to say, seventy feet, and then change directions and cast to a target at fifty feet. He also likes drills that teach you the maximum amount of line you can pick up, so you won't have a back cast crash into the water. Make long casts then learn how much line you can pick up and when to shorten by first stripping in some line. If you'd like a visual guide for length, you can mark your line with a Sharpie at the back of the head or your maximum pick-up point.

EQUIPMENT MAINTENANCE

Fly line performance deteriorates from the accumulation of dirt and from twists and coil memory. Current, forward boat motion, and stripping can cause a fly to spin. A weed on the hook can cause line-damaging twists. Mending in one direction will also put twist in the line.

Storing line on the reel for long periods—especially in high temperatures—will create coil memory. Having an unnecessary snarl ruin a cast to a fish you've invested time in is a disappointing waste. That's why I'm a fanatic about line cleanliness, straightness, and storage. It improves casting immeasurably. If a line has coil memory, you must stretch it out before casting. Trailing a line behind a boat or in a current will straighten twists as long as nothing on the end of it causes it to spin. I believe in washing floating saltwater lines every couple of days with mild soap and water and lubricating them. I still use Glide™ line dressing on all my floating lines. Even though almost all modern fly lines are self-lubricating, I do it anyway. Rods and reels also need periodic care.

When you finish for the day in saltwater, rinse the rods down with a hose at close range, but spare the pressure on the reels. A light sprinkle is all that's needed to help dissolve most of the salt and rinse away sand and the like. Driving contamination into bearings and drags is not a good idea. Once a week fishing in saltwater, I remove the reels and wash them with mild soap, warm water, and a terry cloth. I rinse out the cloth and wipe and re-rinse until the suds are gone. Dry with a towel or chamois. Also, loosen your reel's drag knob after it is clean and dry.

I annually clean my rods by rubbing the guides with WD-40 on a Q-Tip. I spray the reel seat with it and wipe it dry with a paper towel. I run old wax and grime off the male ferrule with a clean paper towel and apply new ferrule wax directly and buff it in with the tip of my index finger. Always check the tightness of your ferrules after a lot of casts. Casting a rod with loose ferrules can damage them.

Storing line tightly on the reel from your last trip can make it difficult to cast them for the first few hours of your next trip. Think how tightly the line is wound from a fight with a big fish. The line coating can conform to the shape of the line under it and leave dents and flat spots. Prevent this after your next trip by stripping out the line and wind it on with little tension.

CHAPTER 7

TROUBLESHOOTING

T his is the section of this book to come to when you are unable to fix something in your cast, or maybe need to understand it a little better. Most faults in casting are in the inability to make a good loop on both front and back casts, and in attaining enough distance. If you try my suggestions and still can't remedy a problem, it's always best to get experienced help.

Faults in a back cast are most common, since they are behind our field of view. It is our weakest casting direction from a strength perspective. I recommend properly watching the back cast when needed. When most people try to see the back cast, they turn their hips a little which turns their shoulder, causing tracking problems. Try to only turn your neck to see your back cast. Seeing the line helps you cast better because you can make real-time corrections. Another way to verify mistakes is with the help of video.

Someone who knows what to look for can examine video at a later time, or view it online, if they are not present when you're casting. With today's technology, you can even upload your video and share the link with a coach thousands of miles away for their analysis.

The current hardware and software solutions for video analysis are devices like the Apple iPad or Android tablets and apps such as UberSense and Coach's Eye. I use Coach's Eye to compare two casters, or to do a before-and-after, using side-by-side video playback. The video scroll wheel lets you clearly show action back and forth

A tablet mounted on a tripod enables you or an instructor to capture and see things in your cast you both might be missing. Photo: Chris Theising.

and at any speed, or cue it to an exact spot. The apps enable you to draw on the screen with your finger and even measure angles. You can use a bracket and tripod or clamp, or your observer can handhold the tablet for capturing the casts. If the screen is too small, or sun is too bright, you can use a video display or wide screen TV indoors.

POOR TIMING

Most timing faults are in the back cast and you should try to identify them by watching. If your back cast has adequate line speed but the line is falling too much, start the forward cast sooner. On the other hand, if you try this and you're cracking the whip by starting too early, watch the end of the line and start a little later, when it's almost straight. Make sure your casting hand stops affirmatively and is still for a perceptible moment in-between casts.

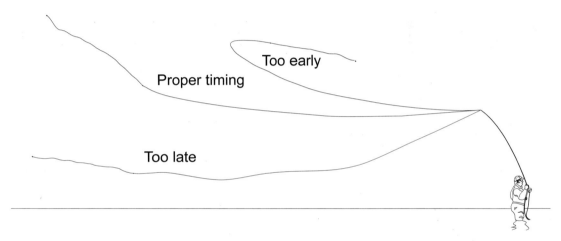

The object in proper back cast timing is to begin the forward cast when the line is almost completely unrolled, but not noticeably falling.

WIDE LOOP FAULT

I consider a wide loop to be a loop measuring greater than four feet wide. If a caster tries to cast a tight loop, and the only result is a wide loop on the forward or back casts, there is a defect in the caster's mechanics, unless there is a mismatch between rod and line.

To identify and correct wide loop faults, note where you stop the rod at the ends of the stroke and use less rod arc as needed. You know you've shortened the stroke too much if you're accelerating smoothly, adhering to the 180-degree angle principle, and suddenly you're casting a tailing loop.

There are three ways to cast a wide loop when making a forward and back cast. The first is to cast with too much rod arc on both casts. If you were to trace through the air with your rod tip, it would look like an igloo. Even prolonging a stop can cause a wide loop without you realizing it. The most common cause of a wide loop is flexing the wrist too much. When you first learn casting, you should limit wrist rotation and mainly use your arm and shoulder.

The caster's wrist in this photo has opened too far on the back cast and will result in a wide loop. Photo: Edina Field.

Once you can cast a good loop at short to medium distances, then learn to add wrist rotation for more speed and distance. When you add wrist movement, you must compensate by slightly reducing arm and shoulder movement. Otherwise, the rod arc and resulting loop will become larger. When you advance and need more line speed and distance, adding wrist movement is imperative.

The second way a caster casts a wide loop is to use too much rod arc on only one of the casts; either the back cast or forward cast. For example, the caster makes a good forward cast, but drops the wrist on the back cast and makes a wide loop. Another fault is when the back cast resembles the letter "L," instead of the letter "J." Delaying and then overpowering rod rotation on the back cast causes this, and directs the end of the loop downward. The remedy is to accelerate the rod smoothly from front to back. Never snap your wrist at the end of a cast.

Another way to make a wide loop is to accelerate a soft rod with "full speed" from beginning to end of the stroke, or stop to stop. The rod will bend too much and the tip will direct the line down in both directions, instead of making casts straight ahead and straight back.

Sometimes, making wide loops becomes habitual. If you have this fault, try using these

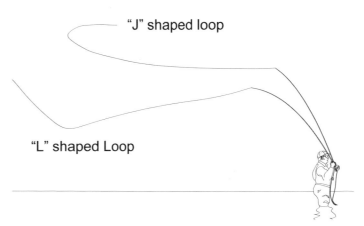

"J" shaped loop

"L" shaped Loop

An efficient loop should look like a "J" not like an "L" when it is unrolling.

cures. One technique to alleviate "wristing" is to squeeze the index and thumb on the grip during the back cast stop of the rod. The muscle contraction temporarily adds some firmness to the wrist. Another technique is to place the reel against the inside of your forearm so you can't use your wrist. Another is to wear a long-sleeve shirt and tuck the rod butt into your cuff to hold it rigid until the new stroke is in your muscle memory. If you still can't break the habit, there is a brace that restricts unwanted motion. One on the market is called The Royal Wulff Wristlok. You can use it until the feeling of a proper stroke becomes automatic.

TAILING LOOP FAULT

In a good loop, the line on the top and on the bottom, should be parallel and in one plane. A tailing loop is a fault because it doesn't fly through the air well, which hurts distance and accuracy. Tailing loops can cause collapsed casts and collisions between the fly and your rod. Tails are usually the cause of overhand knots in the leader, although incomplete leader turnover from wind can also cause them. Regardless of the cause, these knots which weaken the leader are commonly called wind knots.

You can identify a tailing loop when the line from the fly to the front of the loop crosses below the portion of the line from the point of the loop to the rod and there is an upward curve in the line and leader past this intersection. In the worst tailing loop, the fly leg also crosses the rod leg of the loop twice and resembles a figure eight on its side as in the accompanying photo.

An abrupt stroke or haul causes tailing loops. This abruptness causes too much sudden force at some point in the stroke or haul. This error can be made at the beginning of the stroke, the middle, or at the end. The stroke and haul must be properly combined to accelerate the line properly. I'm going to describe four ways to make tailing loops and how to cure each. If you cast a tailing loop, identify how you do it and try my suggestions.

The first and most common way, when everything else is right, is accelerating and bending the rod abruptly at the beginning of the forward stroke. To cure this, accelerate smoothly from the beginning to the end of the cast. Reducing line speed is also a good way to smooth out the stroke. Remember though, whenever you change line speed, always readjust the length of the pause between casts.

This is a close-up of a tailing-loop. Notice that the end of the line and leader are curving upward. Photo: Edina Field.

The second cause of a tailing loop is making a cast with insufficient rod arc. This occurs when the casting stroke is too short. This causes the rod to bend too suddenly and the line follows the rod tip downward and up in erroneous directions. The recommended cure is to add some length to the casting stroke and adhere to the 180-degree principle.

The third cause is "creep." Creep is unintentional movement of the rod hand in the direction of the cast, without acting on the line. This shortens the real start of the stroke, leaving too little to make a good loop. During the pause, don't move your rod hand in the casting direction until the fly line straightens and you start the stroke. To help students prevent creep I tell them to say "freeze" to themselves during the pause.

If that doesn't help, another cure for a tailing delivery cast is to incorporate "drift" after the back-cast stop. Drift is an intentional rearward repositioning movement during the pause to increase potential forward stroke length or arc (see Chapter 5: Distance Casting). The old saying goes, if you're moving backward, you can't be creeping forwards.

The fourth cause of a tailing loop is having enough arc, but slowing the stroke prematurely. It will cause the rod to unbend and straighten prematurely. When it straightens, the tip rises and makes part of the line bounce upward into a tailing loop.

ROD PLANE (TRACKING) FAULTS

As I mentioned earlier, the rod must move through one plane from back to front to make a good loop. If the rod hand—and subsequently the rod—waver in the horizontal plane, the loop will twist in the air. This hurts the aerodynamics of the cast and this loop will probably fail to turn over and straighten. This can rob the cast of massive amounts of distance and accuracy, not to mention create a tangled landing, or worse, hit the caster with the fly.

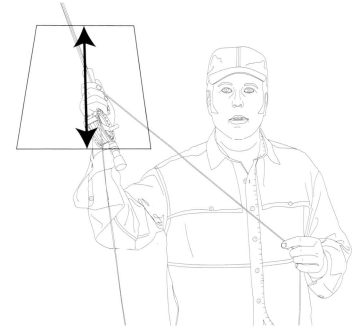

When you extend and retract your arm using the shoulder, elbow, and wrist joints, they must make the correct compound movements or the path of the rod hand won't be straight. This is how we make tracking errors. The farther you bring your casting hand rearward, the harder it will be to track straight. If your hand isn't tracking straight, the rod won't be either. Any motion of the rod hand is multiplied at the rod tip.

Good tracking and well-formed loops depend upon maintaining alignment without side deviation throughout the cast.

One of the biggest causes of poor tracking is excessive wrist rotation in or out on the back cast. Since the rod handle and rod blank are not exactly in line with, or parallel to the forearm when you cast, any forearm twisting will cause an eccentric movement of the rod tip. Although it's good to relax the grip after the stop, many casters let the wrist droop to the side during the stop. This is one place the fault occurs. If you have muscle memory of throwing a ball or swinging a racquet, it might cause curving motions in your casting stroke. For example, we're taught to set up to throw a football with an inward wrist rotation to cock the wrist almost behind the ear and then cross the body on the follow-through after the release.

To find out how straight your tracking is, you can take video of your cast with the camera in front of, or behind the rod, showing the tip. Cast at or above the camera. Casting in front of a mirror or reflective window can also show your tracking. Seeing an error happening in real time can enable you to correct it and practice correct form. Joan Wulff often reminds us to always use real or imaginary targets for both back cast and forward casts to maintain their 180-degree relation to each other.

I think casting up and down a horizontally-outstretched rope or line of targets is the best exercise to cure tracking errors and is a good maintenance drill. The stripes of an athletic field sideline work well visually but you can't move them relative to the wind like you can a rope. You should either cast downwind or with the wind on your non-casting side.

My preference is to arrange four small fluorescent plastic sport cones at twenty-five foot intervals in a straight line one hundred feet long. Place a fifth cone in the middle of the line and stand back so your rod tip is directly over the middle cone when it is held in your normal casting plane. If you don't keep your tip traveling over the imaginary or real line, you will be casting in a long triangle. Now false cast using the cones as targets in front and back. The true test is to just let the back cast land as your delivery without looking at it until it has landed. Now note where it landed, taking any side-wind drift into consideration. If the line lands in line with the cones, super. If not, observe a back cast aiming down the line by only turning your neck—making sure your body isn't

The author is casting over the lines on a field to test his tracking. Correcting tracking problems and casting properly will help your "muscle memory." Photo: Edina Field.

twisted—and look at the alignment of your arm to the target and the angles you need to make the cast. Make a few false casts and retest the back cast until you're tracking straight and true. If you are aware of where your back cast is going and how your loop is unrolling, you can set up for great forward casts.

HAULING FAULTS AND CURES

Even with a good stroke, improper haul timing and acceleration can help cause a tailing loop or slack and the resulting wide loop. As with everything, a haul is either correctly timed, too early, or too late. The correct timing is to haul at the same time as the stroke. Like the stroke, it should also be continuous. If you haul abruptly at the beginning of the stroke, it can help cause a tailing loop. Picking line up off the water is a special case because the stroke is long and delayed by water tension. If your loop is too wide and the back cast is weak when you make a pickup, the haul timing is probably too early. There is probably slack in the pick-up and the rod is not moving the line. If this is occurring, wait until your back cast stroke is half way up before hauling. The problem with hauling too late will be abruptness, a loss of potential line speed and possibly pulling the loop open.

One fault I often see is slack between the line hand and stripper guide on the return move. This is caused by a weak or unnecessarily long haul on the preceding cast, relative to the amount of rod speed. Another similar fault is when a caster tries to return line faster than the cast is unrolling, and the line above the hand loses tension. You can't push slack through the guides. Just slow down the return, or up-stroke of the double-haul. You need sufficient line speed in the cast to pull line back into the guides. The length of the haul should be proportional to the length of the cast; a short haul for a short cast and a long haul for a long cast. A short cast might need a six-inch haul and a really long one might need a four-footer.

Another of the most common hauling faults I see is on the back cast. The caster holds the line in the line hand and makes the back cast but doesn't move the hauling hand. To the caster, it looks like a proper haul is occurring because the hands are separating but the line is sliding through the guides with insufficient speed. As I suggested earlier, move the line hand (with the line) in unison with the casting hand when false-casting without hauling. When you do haul, your line hand will be trained to stay in the proper relationship, ready to make a haul.

Another problem when hauling is tangling line on the rod-butt. Hauling or releasing line under the rod butt is the cause. As line coils tighten, a stray coil can lasso the rod butt. Also, when you make the return in a double-haul with your line-hand below the reel, line can wrap. When you release the line to shoot it, slack will be pulled through the stripping guide, but if anything interrupts the flow of line through the guides, the line reaches out like an octopus and wraps around the rod butt. If these things occur to you, guide the line to the side away from the rod, or haul in a line where your line hand would pass the outside of your thigh. If you make a haul at too great an outward angle, it can cause line resistance and even pull the rod out of plane during a cast.

The remedy for these problems is to learn to use proper mechanics, timing, and smooth acceleration. If you see errors while false casting and hauling, try casting without hauling to determine the cause: Is it the stroke or the haul? Then you can address what is causing the error.

INSUFFICIENT DISTANCE

The cause of a lack of distance is usually inadequate line speed. You can count on one or more shortages in either the amount of hauling, body movement, or stroke length. A collapsed leader instead of a straightened one is a common symptom. First, make sure your loop is tight enough and you're carrying the maximum of amount of line you can without slack. Try releasing the line as early as you can after you stop the rod, so that the rod doesn't pull the loop open as the tip continues bending downward.

If your hauling timing is good, ensure that you make a maximum-length haul and thrust your casting arm on delivery. When you can do these things with your upper body, learn to use your legs and hips for effective weight transfer while false casting and especially on the delivery.

In fishing situations, one mistake many new anglers make is to lower the rod to make their stop on the presentation cast. Instead, they should make the forward stroke longer and a little higher than the preceding one, then lowering the tip after the loop is formed. I watch anglers false cast on my skiff and everything looks great until they make the last cast. I sometimes say when they're false casting, let it go!

CHAPTER 8

ACA CLUBS AND EVENTS

The American Casting Association is the current name of an association of casting clubs that started in 1907. The first name was the National Association of Scientific & Angling Clubs, followed by the National Association of Angling and Casting Clubs, and then it was reborn in 1961 with its current name. The name has gone through an evolution reflecting that of its membership. Its current tax-exempt purpose is to foster amateur national and international casting sport. Our organization has always sanctioned the National Casting Championships and Official National Casting Records. It also trains and sponsors the US Casting Team in international competition. The Association includes Canadian members too, but Canada has its own national casting team that competes abroad. People have joined these clubs because they have wanted to learn how to cast for the benefit it gives to their fishing ability, the comradery, and the enjoyment of competition.

Tournament casting was very popular until the development of the modern spinning reel and anti-backlash bait-casting reels. People didn't need much instruction and practice in order

Some of the Golden Gate Casting Club pools, which are open to the public. Photo: George McCabe.

to use them successfully. Other reasons, such as the ease of traveling to fine fishing as well as cultural changes, also contributed to a decline in this sport, beginning around 1960. But anglers and casters have still needed instruction in fly casting, because it is much more difficult to master than other kinds of fishing. There has been a resurgence in the ACA in recent years and several new clubs have started. Participation in the new World Championships in Fly Casting has also spawned new interest.

The ACA has a rich history of members who've contributed to tackle and casting innovation. Some of its early participants were tackle manufacturers who used tournament casting like today's industrial research and development labs. Techniques for tackle building and casting have been passed down through the generations and have helped develop the talents of casters such as Joan Wulff, brothers Steve and Tim Rajeff, Chris Korich, Henry Mittel, and the latest, Maxine McCormick, an international casting champion at the age of eleven.

The ACA Annual National Championships offers three fly-casting accuracy and three distance games, in addition to six plug events. Each event has its own tackle rules to make the playing field level for competitors. The accuracy events have official target and court rules. This standardization helps with consistency when practicing at home and competing at other ACA Clubs.

These games help us learn and practice a variety of essential skills, which constitute the foundation of successful fly fishing. Within the accuracy games, you must learn how to control line and make line-length adjustments while false casting and aiming from target to target. The distance events are held on the grass of athletic fields in order to accurately judge and measure the casts. Distance competition helps learn skills essential for open-water casting on lakes and in saltwater. ACA accuracy targets are stationary plastic or aluminum hoops, but in fishing, the targets are less obvious and predictable.

The origins of ACA fly games evolved from earlier events cast by competitors of European immigrants in the parks of New York and Chicago. These casters, including women, were mainly accustomed to fishing for trout and salmon. They used all kinds of tackle and fly rods for one- and two-handed casting. On the other hand, the Bass Bug Accuracy event is very American. There has been a trend toward adopting many of the international events so US competitors don't have to prepare to compete in quite so many events.

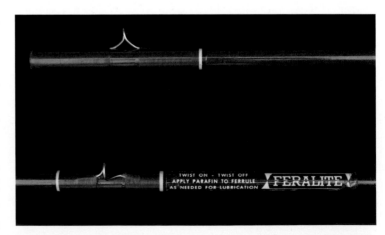

The Ferralite ferrule was invented by ACA caster Jim Green in the 1960s when he was a rod designer at Fenwick Fly Fishing. It was the first non-metallic ferrule and flexes during the bend of the rod.

Most of our distance fly game rules require tackle that is not intended for use in fishing because the lines are too heavy and the rods too stiff. The ACA sells special distance blanks Steve Rajeff has designed at rodmaker G.Loomis for our distance events. They are designed for high-line speed but are only under G.Loomis warranty for tournament casting, since the thin wall construction is not designed to stand up to the strains of fighting fish.

Even in accuracy events, we use a 7-weight line in a dry fly event and today's average trout outfit is a 5-weight. Nevertheless, the old games contain lessons that prepare us for a wide range of freshwater and saltwater fishing pursuits. Below are summaries of the origin, procedure, rules, and some tips on ACA fly accuracy events. Absent are summaries of the extensive Tackle & Equipment Regulations. To see the complete rules, go to americancastingassoc.org.

ACA-RECOGNIZED FLY EVENTS

GENERAL TOURNAMENT RULES

All scoring casts shall be performed from a distinctively marked casting box.
In all distance events, the casting box shall measure six (6) feet square.
In all accuracy events, the casting box shall measure four (4) feet square.

FLY ACCURACY EVENTS

DRY FLY ACCURACY

Dry Fly Accuracy concentrates on turning over the leader properly with the large wind-resistant dry fly without ticking the water. This, of course, is unlike real fishing because you usually do not false cast over wary fish or present as forcefully as you must here.

Procedure
Hold fly—no more than two feet of line extended past tip and all other line on reel.
Unlimited false casts:
Round 1: Present the fly to five targets in order called by Captain
Round 2: Repeat (every caster casts to targets in same order)

Dry Fly Accuracy Technique by Chris Korich
The foundation of your casting form is your stance in relation to the target. Don't change aim from target to target by twisting at the waist. Keep the same upper and lower body relationship for consistency. Start the aiming process by first positioning your feet and the casting stroke will be in alignment.

Next in importance is keeping your stroke slightly to the side of your head so you can see the progress of the loop. This helps the aiming process because it aides your depth perception. Just as you complete your forward stroke with the rod, look up without moving your head and follow the line as it flows toward the target. You'll find with practice that spotting the fly over the target is much easier using this this method than looking for the fly to pop into your field of vision.

Another useful tip involves observing where your fly is landing with respect to the target. Is it consistently long or short? This can be a valuable observation for your remaining shots, for it tells you something about your measuring.

A good caster plays the wind. You will notice that even on the windiest days, especially where it seems to blow in circles, every so often the wind will pause or at least become directionally consistent. Even if this is only for a moment, this is all the time you need. Make your presentation now!

You should also take advantage of long pauses in the wind to move from target to target as fast and accurately as possible. When extending or shortening line between targets, false cast five or six feet above the water. Being that you're not actually attempting a measurement between targets, there's no reason to false

Chris Korich hovering a fly at the first target in the Dry Fly Accuracy event at the Pittsburgh Casting Club.

cast too low and risk a chance of ticking. Once you're trying to measure a cast to a given target, lower your false cast to about two feet.

Don't waste time making unnecessary false casts. Yet, on the other hand, don't rush. There's nothing wrong with using your allotted time. If your hand or arm becomes fatigued, throw the line behind you and rest.

Another observation that's a must on the farthest target: After making your first-round presentation, observe where your fly lands and take notice how much excess line remains hanging from the reel. If you scored perfect, simply extend your line in the second round until the same amount of line extends again. Even if you missed the first-round shot, you should still be able to estimate what would have been the correct amount of line, and hence, have the second round shot pre-measured. (Revised from *The Creel* circa 1979.)

TROUT FLY ACCURACY

Trout Fly Accuracy combines techniques similar to fishing technique. The Dry Fly Round has repetitive false-casting similar to drying-off a dry fly. The Wet Fly round which has two false casts after the first target, is similar to the way we would want to keep a sunken fly in front of the fish and not in the air. The Roll Cast round teaches us how to make fast presentations with limited back cast space and a slight change of direction.

Procedure

Hold fly—no more than two feet of line extended past tip and all other line on reel.

Round 1: Dry Fly—unlimited false casts to targets—first through. Strip in line onto ground.

Hold fly: No more than two feet of line extended etc.

Round 2: Wet fly Round—unlimited false casts to 1st target.

One false cast to second through fifth.

Strip in line to first target.

Round 3: Roll Cast to first target until you hit it. You may strip in line to shorten line out. Extend line by shaking out line and roll cast to two through five, extending line in same manner. (Fifteen casts maximum.)

TROUT FLY ACCURACY BY JOHN FIELD

The same approach that Chris Korich wrote for the Dry Fly event applies to the dry fly round of Trout Fly, and with the exception of the number of allowed false casts in the Wet Fly round, it also applies here too. The hardest round for many is the Roll Cast round because of three things. The first cast is so close, it's difficult to keep the fly in the water while having enough line to form a D-loop. That is why it helps to kneel to create more slack. Secondly, one must change directions in the roll cast up to approximately 45 degrees since the targets are not in a line. This requires making casts over both shoulders and with side winds too.

Third is the degree of difficulty hitting the forty-five to fifty-foot target even with a side or head wind and a change of casting angle. You must set up your cast by dragging all but about the

Chris Korich demonstrating the roll cast kneeling position in the Trout Fly Accuracy event, which helps casting to the first target with a short line.

last four feet of fly line behind you for enough weight to make the cast reach. If dealing with a head wind, you could even point your rod well behind you and keep the rod tip low for maximum power and line control.

During the Roll Casting round of Trout Fly, once you have correct form programmed in your brain, you can almost aim with your toe, close your eyes, and cut the target in half!

BASS BUG ACCURACY

Bass Bug Accuracy is not only good practice for bass fishing, it is also great practice for fishing surface flies to many saltwater species like snook and stripers.

Procedure

Strip out line to at least ten feet past sixth target.

Hold Fly—no more than second feet of line extended past tip.

Round 1: Unlimited false casts to first target, then two false casts to second through sixth targets.

Round 2: Strip in line onto ground. Unlimited false casts to first target, then one false cast to second through sixth targets.

BASS BUG ACCURACY—HENRY MITTEL, CASTING CHAMPION

In all fly accuracy events, the straightest and most reliable way to the center of the target is a tight loop. Every caster should do everything possible to learn to cast extremely tight loops, reliably. But given that nobody is perfect, we have to accept the fact that sometimes our timing isn't perfect, that we get thrown off by the wind just a little. Casts in Bass Bug are especially susceptible to small errors or imperfections. The heavy bug on a short leader easily jerks the line around if we added too much power or didn't use the right timing. This results in waves in the leader and line, which can easily lead to tangles when the loop is super tight. Hence, every caster who hasn't achieved the ability to cast a perfect loop 100 percent of the time has to make a compromise.

On one side, a tight loop delivers the bug more accurately and reliably and one can judge distance better. On the other side, there is the risk of a tangle. That virtually always means the loss of all the points on the next target because of the limited number of available false casts. Every caster should be aware of the number of waves and glitches he/she tends to have. The loop size should be adjusted accordingly. As the caster gets better, this adjustment could depend on the conditions. Under perfect calm, the best loop size should be rather tight, almost like in Dry Fly. Under windy conditions, especially when the wind isn't constant, the caster would probably open up the loop to be safer. Ideally, one would open up the loop only for casts where there's trouble during the backcast and only proportionally to the amount of trouble there really is.

This photo shows the ACA Bass Bug with a tippet ready to loop on in case one is damaged in a round.

Steve Rajeff is false casting to the far target in the ACA Bass Bug Accuracy event.

One more thing about tight loops in Bass Bug: They are especially desirable during false casts. A tight loop shoots line better than an open loop because of higher line speed. Also, the bug doesn't move as quickly when the line and leader are practically straight. That makes it easier to judge the distance, which is very important, especially in the second round when we only have one chance. The tight loop is somewhat less important during the lay-down cast. If the bug moves fast as the line and leader become straight, this only affects how fast the bug will hit the water. That is, unless you plan on judging distance also on the lay-down for last minute corrections. Those last-second corrections should be common knowledge for casts to the sixth target. However, they can be applied to a lesser extent also for the fifth and fourth target too.

FLY DISTANCE EVENTS

Angler's Fly Distance—Fly Distance Singlehanded—Fly Distance Doublehanded: The rules of the fly distance events are similar except for equipment, allowable time, and the use of a line tender. The equipment is described by event. The Distance Course, Method of Casting (with exceptions noted), and Method of Scoring are described collectively.

Distance Course: The Distance Course shall be a court of sufficient length with a maximum width of 180 degrees and a minimum width of one hundred feet at a distance of two hundred feet. Both the left and right court boundaries shall be marked before the event begins. The marking should consist of ropes, or tape secured to the ground, or a series of clearly visible stakes or flags.

General: Time starts when caster calls "score" or at the expiration of the two (2) minute preparation time. Caster must call "score" before the fly passes the casting box on the way forward for a shooting cast.

Caster's Score: The caster's longest shooting cast shall constitute the caster's score. The second longest shooting cast shall be recorded, but shall be used only to break ties.

Angler's Fly Distance: Angler's Fly Distance, also known as steelhead distance, came from the West Coast steelheaders who use sinking heads for maximizing casting distance and control of presentation depth. They use floating, intermediate and sinking heads. Angler's Fly Distance only uses a sinking tournament head. Winning distances at a National average 175 feet today. The Official National record at the time of this printing is 192 feet.

Caster may have a "Gillie" to help remove line from reel and straightening line, which begins the two-minute preparation time. After that, the Gillie cannot assist in any way. The time limit for Angler's Fly Distance: Five minutes.

Singlehanded Fly Distance: Five (5) minutes. Tender (Gillie) can assist to extend and stretch the line during the two-minute prep time. After that, the Gillie cannot assist in any way.

Doublehanded Fly Distance: Seven (7) minutes. Fly Distance Double-handed a line. Tender (Gillie) can assist to extend and stretch the line and retrieve line as needed during prep time and during the round.

SPECIAL EVENTS

In addition to the six Recognized fly events, there are also three additional fly Special Events that may be held. These events are: ACA Skish Fly Accuracy, Wet Fly Accuracy, and 5-Weight Combination Accuracy and Distance Event. I've included the whole official rules (as of this printing) for the 5-weight event because it's relatively new and is gaining in popularity. Its object is to encompass both disciplines and use commonly available fishing tackle.

ACA 5 wt. Combination Accuracy and Distance—Special Event Rules:

1. GENERAL

    The 5wt Combination event consists of accuracy and distance casting with a 5-weight line. The accuracy and distance parts may be cast as separate event(s) according to the following rules and regulations.

2. EQUIPMENT

    A) Rod – Rod length shall not exceed nine feet (9') overall. A measurement tolerance of one inch (1") shall be permitted. Only one rod may be used during the course of the event unless the judge declares a damaged rod as unusable.

    B) Reel – Unrestricted, must be attached to the rod for all scoring casts. The line and leader and any backing used to compete in the event must fit completely onto the reel and must be carried on the reel prior to the event.

    C) Line – The line shall consist of optional, unrestricted backing and a floating, weight-forward fly line that meets the following specifications (recommended Lines):

        i)   Length – The fly line must be at least eighty-eight feet long. The front eighty-eight feet must be one piece and free of splices.

        ii) Running line – The part of the fly line between forty-two feet and eighty-eight feet from the tip is considered running line. It must be level except for manufacturing tolerances. The diameter of the running line may not be less than 0.031 inches and not more than 0.037 inches.

   iii)   Head – The head is the heavy front part of the weight-forward fly line including the tip section and all tapers. The head must be thirty-five feet to forty-two feet long, i.e., the diameter of the level running line must be reached no less than thirty-five feet and no more than forty-two feet from the tip of the fly line.

   iv)   Weight – The mass of the first forty feet of the fly line plus the mass of the leader shall not exceed 12.50 grams (193 grains).

   v)   Specific gravity – All parts of the fly line must be of floating material.

      The line shall meet the above specifications without stretching after it is stripped from the reel for verification by tournament officials.

D)   Leader – Shall be constructed of monofilament with a minimum of seven feet and a maximum of 9 ½ feet in length with a maximum tippet diameter of .009 inches (including any knots) and minimum tippet length of eighteen inches. The length of the leader is measured from the tip of the fly line to the eye of the fly.

E)   Fly – A single tournament dry fly with hackle not less than and not more than one inch in diameter may be attached to the leader at the tip end. An attached or lost fly may be replaced at any time with a fly approved by the judge.

3.   COURSE

A)   Accuracy – A square casting box four feet on each side and five targets shall constitute the course. The course may be laid out on any suitable casting surface such as water, grass, or carpet. The casting box may be at the same level as the targets and, if elevated, should not be higher than 18″. Each target consists of two concentric rings with outer diameters of thirty inches and fifty-four inches. The ring cross section shall be no more than 1.5 inches. The outer ring must not have a cross section larger than the inner ring. Each target shall be secured in place so that the total movement for any reason will not exceed one foot in any direction. The first target shall be centered in front of the casting box at a distance of twenty to twenty-five inches. The second target—called the obstacle target—shall be located directly behind and touching the first target. The third and fourth targets shall be at a distance of thirty-five to forty feet and forty-five to fifty feet, respectively. The fifth target—called the bonus target—shall be at a distance of sixty to eighty feet, depending on the level of the competition.

B)   Distance – The casting box used for distance has the same dimensions as the box for accuracy. If accuracy and distance are cast as a combination, one and the same box is used for both. The distance will be measured along a real or imagined centerline extending perpendicularly from the front edge of the casting box. The space available for landing the fly—the casting lane—must extend at least five feet to each side of that centerline. Lines perpendicular to the centerline, or other means that do not obstruct the casting nor the retrieval of line, may be used to mark certain distances and to determine the position of the fly to the nearest foot.

4. TIME
    A) General – Each caster shall be allotted time for preparing for the event and time for casting the event.
    B) Preparation time – Preparation time starts when the judge has called up the caster and declared the casting box as "open". The caster may use prep time to strip line off the reel and arrange it on the ground in any practical way—with or without assistance. Preparation time ends when one minute expires or the caster declares readiness for start, whichever occurs first.
    C) Casting time – The time allotted for casting the 5-weight combination shall be five minutes. If accuracy is cast as a separate event, the allotted time shall be three minutes. If distance is cast as a separate event, the allotted time shall be three minutes. The following procedure shall be used to start the casting time. When the caster appears to be ready for the event, but not later than fifty seconds after the beginning of prep time, the judge shall ask: "Caster ready?" Upon a positive reply from the caster or when one minute of prep time has expired, the judge begins the casting time by calling "Start." No score can be obtained from casts completed after the casting time has expired. A cast counts as completed during casting time when the forward motion of the rod has stopped before time expires.
    D) Time Out – There shall be no time out for any reason except for outside interference as determined by the Judge. The judge shall only consider unusual interfering circumstances such as third persons, pets, or trees in the course or in the back-cast area as outside interference.

5. METHOD OF CASTING
    A) Combination – The 5-weight-combination casting program consists of the accuracy and distance casting as described in sections 6 and 7. A caster must complete all accuracy casts before any distance casts may be scored. There is no time-out or break between the accuracy and distance parts.
    B) Casting Style – Unrestricted.
    C) Definitions
        i)   A caster is considered in the casting box when at least one foot is on or above the casting box and no part of the caster or any attached clothing touches the surface in front of the casting box.
        ii) When the intact line, leader, and fly settle on the surface or targets in front of the casting box, it shall be considered a final forward cast.

6. ACCURACY
    A) Initial – The caster must begin while meeting the following four conditions simultaneously:
        i)   The caster is in the box.
        ii) Caster does not hold loose line in any way that could indicate distance to any target.

iii)   No more than two feet of fly line are extended beyond the rod tip.

iv)   The caster holds the fly in hand. No final forward cast will count as a scoring cast until the caster has met all four conditions simultaneously during casting time as determined by the judge.

B)   Target order – After meeting the initial conditions, the caster shall make a total of eight (8) final forward casts at the targets in the following order: first target, third target, fourth target, first target, obstacle target, third target, fourth target, and bonus target.

C)   Scoring – Each final forward cast shall be scored where the fly first strikes the casting surface, any portion of a target, or the platform in front of the casting box, regardless of where the fly may ultimately settle. The casting surface inside of the center ring and any part of the center ring above the casting surface scores 500 points. The casting surface between the center ring and the outer ring and any part of the outer ring above the casting surface scores 300 points. Anything outside the outside ring scores 100 points.

D)   Total Score – The total score for accuracy is the sum of the scores achieved on all targets, at which the caster has cast during casting time, minus the sum of all assessed penalties. In a 5-weight combination event, this accuracy score will be added to the distance score.

E)   Penalties – Penalties are assessed towards the score on the next target at which the caster is supposed to cast. Multiple penalties may be assessed as appropriate. The sum of all such penalties shall be limited to the score achieved at that target. The penalties are:

i)   Tick – Should the line extended beyond the rod tip, the leader, or the fly strike the casting surface in front of the casting box or any target when no final forward cast was performed, it shall be scored a tick. The penalty for a tick shall count during the entire casting time, whether caster is in or out of casting box and whether or not the fly is on. The penalty for each tick shall be 10 percent of the score achieved on the next target.

ii)   Obstacle target – The objective when casting at the obstacle target is to have the line and leader settle without crossing any part of the first target—the obstacle. In case the caster fails to meet that objective, the following penalties are assessed: 400 points if the settled line or leader crosses the inner ring of the first target, 200 points if the settled line or leader crosses the outer ring the outer ring, but not the inner ring, of the first target.

iii)   Out-of-the-box – A penalty equal to the entire score achieved on the target shall be assessed if the caster performs a final forward cast without being in the box.

iv)   Illegal strip – A penalty equal to the entire score achieved on the next target shall be assessed if the caster measures line along the rod.

    v)   Early retrieve – A penalty equal to the entire score achieved on the target shall be assessed if the caster lifts the fly off the casting surface after making a final forward cast before the judge calls "score."

    vi)   Lost fly – No penalty shall be assessed for the loss of a fly or for a lost fly falling onto the casting surface. A lost or attached fly may be replaced at any time with a fly approved by the judge.

7.   DISTANCE

  A)   General – When the casters transitions from the accuracy part to the distance part in a combination event or when the caster begins a distance-only event, no special conditions (such as those required for the accuracy part) need to be met.

  B)   SCORING – The point where the fly first strikes the casting surface in front of the casting box during a final forward cast is used to determine the distance of that cast. All distances are measured along the real or imagined centerline extending perpendicularly from the front edge of the casting box. A real or imaginary square is placed such that one edge is on the centerline and the other edge crosses the spot where the fly first struck the casting surface. The distance of the cast is the distance between corner of the square and the front edge of the casting box. The distance shall be determined accurate to the nearest foot. The score is the number of feet times ten (10).

  C)   Number of casts – The caster is permitted to make any number of casts during the allotted time. In a 5wt combination event, the scores of the best two casts will be kept and the sum of their scores will be added to the accuracy score. In a distance-only event, the two best casts will be kept. The caster's longest cast is used to determine the score. The second longest cast shall be recorded, but is only used to break a tie. If a tie still exists, the cast-off procedure described below will be used.

  D)   Penalties

    i)   Ticks – There are no penalties for ticks.

    ii)   Out of the box – If a caster performs a final forward cast without being in the box, the cast is invalid and has a zero score.

    iii)   Out of bounds – If a cast was directed such that the fly cannot land on the casting surface, the cast is invalid and has a zero score.

    iv)   Early retrieve – If a caster retrieves line before the judge calls "score," the cast is invalid and has a zero score.

    v)   Lost fly – No penalty shall be assessed for the loss of a fly or for a lost fly falling onto the casting surface.

8.   CAST-OFFS

In case of a tie for any place earning an award such as prizes or medals, cast-offs shall be performed to determine the final order. The rules for the cast-offs differ slightly from the regular event rules as outlined in the following.

ACA - 5 wt. Combination Special Event									
Caster:						**Class:**			**Date:**
Target	**1**	**3**	**4**	**1**	**2**	**3**	**4**	**5**	**Totals**
Score									+
Penalty									-
Distance	**(feet x 10)**		**(feet x 10)**		**(feet x 10)**		**Score Best 2**		+
									+
Scorekeeper:							**Final Score**		

The scorecard for the ACA 5-Weight Combination Accuracy & Distance event.

ACA Leader Formulas

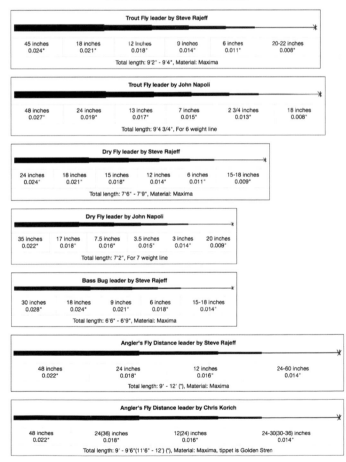

Several winning hand-tied leaders for the Fly Accuracy games and Angler's Fly Distance. The full formulas, including One-Handed and Two-Handed Fly Distance, are on the ACA website.

A) Combination Event – The casters are given two minutes of casting time to perform the following casts: accuracy casts at the first target, the obstacle target, the third target, the fourth target, and the fifth target, then any number of distance casts of which only the best cast is added to the cast-off score. The general procedure including prep time and initial conditions remains unchanged.

B) Accuracy Event – No changes to the event rules apply. Tied casters cast again until the tie is broken.

C) Distance Event – The casters are given one minute of casting time to perform one cast. The longer cast wins. The general procedure including prep time remains unchanged.

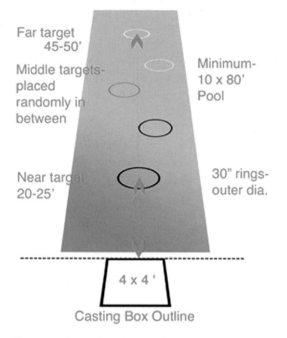

The course layout for ACA Trout Fly and Dry Fly Accuracy. If you add a sixth target at seventy to seventy-five feet, you'll also have the course for Bass Bug Accuracy.

JOINING AND GETTING IN TOUCH WITH THE ACA

The following can help you learn on your own, in conjunction with an instructor or mentor. We have found it be to be the most natural way to achieve good results and cast with the least fatigue. From the Catskills to the Pacific, sixteen ACA clubs and their members are ready to welcome you and share more than one hundred years of casting knowledge. Several of the clubs have concrete ponds with floating targets dedicated to casting. You can find ACA online at americancastingassoc.org.

ACA MEMBER CLUBS

- **Pittsburgh Casting Club**—Pittsburgh, Pennsylvania (eddiefishon@yahoo.com)
- **Scotto Fly Fishing Club**—Ontario, Canada
- **Southern Brothers Casting Club**—Cleveland, Tennessee
- **Catskill Mountains Casting Club**—Livingston Manor, New York (per2@comcast.net)
- **Rio Salado Casting Club**—Tempe, Arizona (http://phoenixflycastersflyfishingarizona.blogspot.com)
- **Blue Grass Sportsmen's League**—Lexington, Kentucky (http://bgslinc.com)
- **Chicago & Valparaiso Casting Club**—Chicago, Illinois (j.sero@comcast.net)

- **Cincinnati Casting Club**—Cincinnati, Ohio (cincinnaticastingclub@gmail.com)
- **Golden Gate Casting & Angling Club**—San Francisco, California (http://www.ggacc.org)
- **Long Beach Casting Club**—Long Beach, California (https://www.longbeachcastingclub.org)
- **Oakland Casting Club**—Oakland, California (https://www.oaklandcastingclub.org)
- **Flycasters**—San Jose, California (http://www.flycasters.org)
- **Scarborough Fly and Bait Casting Club**—Scarborough, Ontario, Canada (http://pages.pathcom.com/~coachman/)
- **Seattle Casting Club**—Seattle, Washington (slowsnap@att.net)
- **Backcountry Fly Fishers**—Naples, Florida (http://www.flyfishingnaples.com)
- **Toledo Casting Club**—Toledo, Ohio (Frank Gralak 419-297-0129)
- **Toronto Sportsmen's Association**—Toronto, Ontario, Canada (http://www.torontosportsmens.ca)

CHAPTER 9

EXERCISES FOR DISTANCE CASTING

Most casters could use better hand speed and stability, and it's the wrists and forearms that most affect hand speed. Below are a few exercises that only work the forearms and wrists. Use these if you feel your forearms are lagging behind the rest of your body. Be careful not to overtrain them! If you'd like the benefit of seriously training your whole body as a distance competitor might, then also read the section following this one. Warm up and stretch before and after exercises. Only perform these workouts with approval of your physician.

FOREARM WORKOUTS

Barbell Wrist Curls

Use a light weight. Have your palms facing up. Keep your elbows stationary on a bench or on your knees while sitting. Most bodybuilders use a rep range between twelve and fifteen. Experiment to see what works best for you.

Reverse Wrist Curls

Same as the Barbell Wrist Curl except with a reverse palms-down grip. Use a light weight. Keep your elbows stationary on a bench or on your knees while sitting.

Massive Forearm Scorcher

Superset all the below back-to back without resting in between.

1. Vertical Wrist Rotations with Light Dumbbell (ten to twenty-five pounds): one minute
    Standing up straight. Feet slightly apart. Arms hanging at sides with sufficient space to rotate dumbbells. Hands holding dumbbells in same style as holding a dip bar at full extension. Rotate left and right wrists simultaneously as great of an angle as possible for one minute.
2. Horizontal Wrist Rotations with Light Dumbbell (ten to twenty-five pounds): one minute
    Immediately after finishing step 1 above. Raise to parallel with the floor and force upper arms and elbows against body (arms should be like holding ski poles). Rotate left and right wrists simultaneously as great of an angle as possible for one minute.

3.   Behind Back Wrist Curl (Use Olympic Bar from Squat Cage or Similar): Thirty Repetitions.

4.   Reverse Arms Curls (Hopefully can use the same bar from step 3).

5.   Seated Palm-Up Wrist Curl with Bar: Thirty Repetitions.

6.   Seated Palm-Down Wrist Curl with Bar: Thirty Repetitions.

7.   Hammer Curls, Alternating Left and Right Arms (Total of Ten or So Repetitions per Arm).

Repeat 1–7. Stretch after exercises.

FULL BODY DISTANCE WORKOUT

DAY 1: Warm-up & Stretch before Exercises:

Triceps: Twelve sets: Pull-downs, skull crushers, kick-backs, dips.

Biceps: Fourteen sets curls.

Forearms: Hammer curls, wrist rolls, horizontal and vertical wrist rotations, stretch after exercises.

DAY 2: Warm-up and stretch before exercises.

Chest: Twelve sets: (Two set warm-up) multi-angle chess press, flat-bench flyes, cable cross-overs. Options: Push-ups.

Glutes and legs: Leg extension, leg curl, leg press, stretch after exercises.

DAY 3: Warm-up and Stretch before exercises:

Back: Twelve sets: chin-ups or *latissimus dorsi* pull-down, bent-over row (barbell), dumbbell rows, hyper-extensions. Options: seated cable row and Abs-crunch & oblique machine, hanging leg lifts, stretch after exercises.

DAY 4: Warm-up and stretch before exercises:

Shoulders: Twelve sets (Two-set warm-up) four sets-military press, side lateral raises, two sets—front raises, seated bent-over lateral raises.

Glutes and legs: Leg extension, leg curl, leg press, stretch after exercises.

DAY 5–7: Aerobic activities like jogging, skiing, hiking etc. Eat healthy and rest well!

GLOSSARY

180-degree principle: In a straight-line cast, the back cast should be 180-degrees opposite the forward cast.

Action: The flex characteristic of a rod or rod blank. Terms including fast, slow, and soft describe action.

Anchor: The line, leader, and fly placed on the water with which, in combination with the resistance of a D-loop, is used to cast the rod in a Spey or roll cast.

Casting cycle: One cycle is comprised of two continuous casts in opposite directions.

Casting Fault: An action or inaction that has a negative effect on an intended cast.

Casting stroke: The path of the rod hand during a cast.

Centripetal force: The resistance required for a rotating object in motion to continue in a curved path, rather than a linear one.

Closed loop: When gravity causes the fly leg to cross the rod leg during a cast, the loop appears closed from the side.

Coil Memory: The propensity of a line to retain the shape of its storage or reel spool, after it is unspooled.

Creep: The forward or backward rod-hand movement during the pause in the direction of the next cast without sufficient movement to bend the rod.

D-Loop: The shape of an unaccelerated backcast of a water anchored cast, such as a Spey or roll cast.

Dead-drift: When a fly travels at the same speed as the current in which it is carried.

Deflection: The amount of bend in a rod or blank held in a fixture at a given angle, caused by a test weight hung from the tip.

Deflection board: A Board or paper sheet mounted behind a rod or blank on which to record deflection with a writing instrument.

Distal grip: A grip with the index finger extended on the handle. It is also known as a three-point-grip.

Double-haul: Making haul and return cycles on successive casts to accelerate the line.

Drag (fly): The effect on the fly when current pulls on the line or leader and moves it at a different speed than the current in which it drifts.

Drift (fly): The effect of current on a fly when it is presented in or on the water.

Drift (rod): Rearward repositioning of the rod after loop formation on the back cast.

False cast: A cast made without delivering the fly. It may be used to dry a fly, extend line or aim.

Fluorocarbon: A clear abrasion resistant fishing line manufactured from extruded polyvinylidene fluoride.

Fly leg: The portion of line and leader from the point of a loop, to the fly, or end of the leader.

Graphite: A material used in modern fly rods and manufactured as a fiber cloth to be wound around a steel mandrel. It is usually impregnated with an epoxy resin that is activated in an oven.

Gulper: A fish, usually a trout, cruising a stillwater in pursuit of insects on the surface.

Haul: A timed tug on the line to accelerate the line during the cast or flight of a loop.

Hover: A technique to increase the visibility of an accuracy false cast by letting the leader straighten over the target for an instant.

Loop: In the words of Bruce Richards, "The shape of an aerialized fly line formed by a casting stroke." Or the "J" shape of a fly line after it has been made airborne by a casting stroke or snap and then sharply decelerated.

Mend: A manipulation of the line after the rod stop of a cast.

Off shoulder: A position with the rod tip over the opposite shoulder from the rod hand.

Overhang: The amount of running or shooting line extended past the tip before delivering a cast.

Over-line: To use a line with a heavier stated weight than stated for the rod, or matched by testing.

Parallel Loop: A loop whose parts are in the same plane and whose fly and rod legs are parallel

Rod Angle: The angle of a rod at a given time in relation to level and to the direction of the cast.

Rod arc: The change in rod butt angle from the beginning of the rod bending to rod straightening as the result of the stroke.

Rod leg: The portion of line being cast from the rod tip to the loop point.

Rod Plane: The planar path of a rod during a cast.

Rod Stop: A term used to describe the deceleration of a fly rod. A fast, complete stop is called a positive stop.

Roll cast: A water anchored cast with no, or a slight change of direction.

Rotation: The angular movement of the rod butt caused by the rod hand.

Running line: A thinly coated line sharing the same core as the head.

Shoot: To extend the length of line beyond the tip by releasing line at the rod stop, letting the cast pull line through the guides.

Shooting head: A head component usually with a rear loop for connecting a shooting line.

Shooting line: (Noun) A thin diameter line attached to a shooting head as part of an interchangeable component system.

Single-haul: A pull and return, or pull and shoot, used on either a single forward cast or back cast.

Stroke: The acceleration and path of the rod hand during a cast.

Stop Sequence: The process of the deceleration of the fly rod and the movement of the rod.

Tailing Loop: A closed loop with an upward curvature of the fly leg which often crosses the main leg a second time.

Tempo: The time between casting cycles.

Timing: The pause between the rod stop and the start of the next cast.

Tippet: Thin diameter of leader tied to fly to avoid visual detection by fish

Tracking: The rod's adherence to one plane during a cast.

Trajectory (casting): The angle of the cast relative to level.

Triangulation: To aim a cast using the perceived distance relationship of the fly, line and leader, rod hand and rod to a target.

ACKNOWLEDGMENTS

Macauley Lord, brothers Steve and Tim Rajeff, Henry Mittel, Chris Korich, Joan Salvato Wulff, the American Casting Association, Chris Thiesing, Sekhar Bahadur, and my wife, Edina Field, for her support and photography.

INDEX

A

Accuracy, 47–52
Assembly, 14–17

B

Backing, 8–9
Bait and switch, 4
Barbell wrist curls, 99
Basket, stripping, 65–66
Bass Bug Accuracy, 88–89
Belgian cast, 51–52

C

Carrying line, 54
Casting
    Belgian cast, 51–52
    body in, 59–61
    Change-of-Direction cast, 51–52
    distance, 53–63
    distance stroke in, 55–58
    false casts, 25, 35
    fan, 4
    fishing casts, 65–73
    games, 43
    ground, 44–45
    horizontal, 44–45
    with kids, 42–45
    in moving water, 67–70
    roll cast, 31–34
    saltwater quick cast, 70–72
    wind casts, 39–42, 53–55
    Wye cast, 52
Casting stroke, 22–23
Change-of-Direction cast, 51–52
Chumming, 4
Cigar, 5

Clicker, 6–7
Compound taper, 8
Conventional fishing, fly casting vs., 1–2
"Cut the Cake," 50

D

Depth control, in moving water, 67–70
Disassembly, 14–17
Distance casting, 53–63. *See also* Casting
Distance faults, 82
Distance stroke, 55–58
Distance training, 62–63
D-loop, 31–34
Double-haul, 36–38, 59
Double-haul false cast drill, 38
Double taper, 8
Dry Fly Accuracy, 85–86

E

Equipment maintenance, 72–73
Exercises, 99–100

F

False casts, 25, 35
Fan casting, 4
Field, John, 87
Fishing casts, 65–73
Fluorocarbon, 10
Fly Distance Events, 89–90
Fly-rod outfit parts, 50
Forearm workouts, 99–100
Full-wells, 5

G

Games, casting, 43
Grip, 23–24
Ground casting, 44–45

H

Half-wells, 5
Handle shapes, 5
Hauling faults, 81–82
Hauling line, 36–39
Head, 8
Horizontal casting, 44–45

K

"Kentucky Windage," 50
Kids, casting with, 42–45
Korich, Chris, 23, 28, 42–43, 47–48, 49, 62,
    85–86

L

Label, on rod, 6
Leaders, 9–10
Lengthening, 35–36
Line connections, 10–12
Line control, 29–30
Line manufacture and design, 7–9
Line threading, 6
Line weights, 2, 7–8
Loop, 24–25

M

Maintenance, 72–73
Massive forearm scorcher, 99–100
Mittel, Henry, 88–89
Moving water, depth and speed control in,
    67–70

N

Nylon, 10

O

Off-Shoulder roll cast, 33
180-degree principle, 25–26

P

Palming rim, 7
Pick-up and lay-down, 34

R

Rajeff, Steve, 37, 50
Rajeff, Tim, 13, 43, 48, 72
Rear taper, 8
Reel parts, 6–7
Release, and shooting line, 59
Reverse wrist curls, 99
Rod, 2–3
Rod arc, 24–25
Rod length, 12–13
Rod plane, 24
Rod plane faults, 79–81
Rod stop, 24
Roll cast, 31–34

S

Saltwater quick cast, 70–72
Shooting heads, 61
Shooting line
    with hauls, 38–39
    release and, 59
Shortening, 35–36
Sight fishing, 4
Single-haul, 36–38
Sizes, 1
Slow-action rod, 3
Speed control, in moving water, 67–70
Stance, 22, 48, 49, 59–61
Stripper guide, 6
Stripping basket, 65–66
Stripping line in, 3
Stroke, 21–22, 22–23, 55–58
Structure fishing, 4

T

Tailing loop fault, 78–79
Tapers, 7–8
Teasing, 4
Tempo, 27
Timing, 27, 76
Tracking faults, 79–81

Trajectory, 26–27, 53–55
Triangle taper, 8
Troubleshooting, 75–82
Trout Fly Accuracy, 86–87

V
V-grip, 23

W
Western tournament style, 21
Wet Fly Accuracy (game), 17, 43, 51

Wide loop fault, 76–78
Wind casts, 39–42
Workouts, 99–100
Wulff, Joan, 44, 48
Wye cast, 52

X
X system, 9